BULLY

Cassandra Grodd

ISBN: 9781730986307

Written by Cassandra Grodd
Illustrations by Raaya Paathare
Edited by Rebekah Bogardus Editing
Edited by James Mckinnon
Design Concept by Cassandra Grodd
Design support by Nika Januszkiewicz
Paperback formatting by Access Ideas

*To anyone who has ever been
their own worst enemy,
this one's for you.*

Contents

To My Readers,

I have written multiple stories for many, many years, and now it is time for me to pass them on to you. They hold a lot of meaning. In order to find the one that you seek, you must first be at real peace with yourself. Love is a reflection of your ability to open up your heart to someone who wants to share your life and experiences, watch you grow, and grow with you. Until you are prepared to allow this to happen, you will keep looking. Real loving is an inside job, and the right person will only reflect what is inside you.

You are a beautiful person, and you have made my entire life meaningful just by holding this book in your hands. I seriously appreciate you – you deserve everything great on this earth, and I am excited for what's in store for you. I know it will be more than you could ever imagine.

You have not found this book by chance. It has found you because it is your time – your time to let go of the hurt, and your time to heal.

I hope the following pages can help you do just that.

Love,
Cass xx

Part One

It's All
in Your Head

I was once given very good advice. As a young writer, I was told you must write about what you are most afraid of. Subsequently, it has taken me eight years to write about this topic. The name of this book was inspired by the story I am about to tell you through the following pieces, and thus, this collection is divided into sections that I hope you will be able to put together in order to understand the puzzle I am presenting to you.

I have encountered some cruel people during my time, but *she* has to have been the worst bully of them all. I think it's because I could never escape her. She stayed as a shadow behind me, a voice running parallel to my conscience, and a parrot on my shoulder – yes, she talked and taunted me for nearly a decade. The worst part about it is that barely anyone knows the extent she went to. Well, actually … no one knows. It wasn't until a few years ago when her voice became too loud and my actions were so obvious that my family noticed. The majority of my friends don't know still to this day. It hurts me that this story will hurt them. I want to apologise for lying, for hiding, and for covering it up. I only did so to protect you because I love you. You love me, but I have never loved myself. I would start this story from the beginning, but I am honestly unsure when it truly began, so let's jump around a bit. Here goes nothing … the only topic I've never talked about … the black box in my mind … my best kept secret … my most embarrassing trait … my unwanted best friend … my untold story – until now.

When you're younger, you are told to tell a trusted adult or teacher if you are being bullied...

But what happens when the bully is in your head?

Bulimia

It was 7,000 feet in the air aboard a Boeing 707 while looking down the sterile, basic, boring, and astronaut-esque airplane toilet that I realised I had a real issue. Not a private-school, upper-class, go-to-a-spiritual-healer-and-become-a-vegan-with-a-blog issue, but a disgusting, raw, filthy, and unacceptable issue. Yes, I was purposely throwing up food I had just paid for on a flight from New Zealand to London. Since I had just parted ways with my family, friends, and life as I knew it, I was now parting ways with some actually half-decent penne pasta and an ice cream pottle. Not one other person on this plane had an issue with the meal, apart from me – great. It wasn't that the food had made me feel sick, and it wasn't that it was undercooked. I wasn't even that full. It was much more than that, and the penne pasta should not be held accountable for the tsunami of guilt that washed over me the second I finished eating it.

That guilt has manifested itself since I was thirteen, almost as if it became a permanent charm bracelet which I had attached multiple charms to over the years. In this bathroom, high above the middle of the Pacific Ocean, fear, insecurity, and pain swung from that guilt-coated chain which glimmered perfectly under the artificial lights at the back of the plane. I sniffed, wiped my eyes, and then initiated a loud flush of the toilet at the same time so no one could hear me dry retch again. God, I love that toilets flush! How weird is that? But fuck, if I met the inventor of the flush, I'd shake his hand. It's one of the only times in my life I could press a button and watch a bad decision disappear.

"That's it – that's the last time!" I said to my red, watery-eyed reflection as my body shook slightly with the turbulence. It was a sentence I would later repeat like a broken record another two times during that flight alone. Here's the best bit – and it makes no sense … I really mean *zero* sense … like minus 100 on a sense-making scale – your body *needs* to eat in order to function, to even keep breathing. The other thing here is that I'm not dumb. Don't let my half-naked Instagram photos or my overpriced blonde highlights fool you. I've obtained a degree, studied internationally, interned, and worked my ass off my entire adult life. I know right from wrong, but this behaviour has kept my life in the wrong for such a long time that it now just feels right. And just like any bad decision facing humanity, it has been repeated.

I can't tell you when the first time was, and I don't even know how I got the idea. I wish I could blame some friend or foe – even a celebrity, but I think I came up with this one all on my own. However, I can tell you when it became a habit – the ripe age of 13 when I found myself in the habit of binge-eating three packets of biscuits, a punnet of ice cream, and four family-size blocks of chocolate … and then spending an hour in the bathroom. But I'd also found myself a couple of identifiers too. Along with weighing in a solid three-to-six kilograms more than all my friends (which mentally felt like over three hundred - honestly, if I'd had it my way, I would have signed myself up for the *Biggest Loser*), I also had one pimple too many, some form of mousey brown hair, pretty questionable fashion sense *cough Ed Hardy cough*, and a passion for horse riding and sticker books. Let's just say, I wasn't exactly Miss Popular.

Amongst the cool skinny girls – whose mums bought them Victoria's Secret bikinis and seemed to ignore the fact that their daughters weren't just on the pill for their skin – was one girl who seemed to float between tween-Queen, short-shorts-wearing machine, and a genuine, smiley, warm person. I'm sure I was some sort of charity case, but we formed a tight friendship, and I could see a part of my soul reflected in her eyes. She told me about a blog she ran (Tumblr, if you care) which no one else knew about. I remember loading it that night and not shutting down my computer until around 3 a.m. Her whole blog was centred around eating, ways to eat, how to eat, and binging – altogether being what is known today as "pro-ana".

It hadn't clicked yet that maybe skinny girls didn't all just come from Skinnyville where they were all skinny together and talked about being skinny all day long. Maybe they too were really worried, and maybe – just maybe – they hurt themselves and were as unhappy about their bodies as I was. Lightbulb moment. Unfortunately, it was a moment that wouldn't make my all-girl private school any easier for "Little-Miss-I-Don't-Fit-In Cass" or "I-Need-to-Wash-My-Hair-More Cass".

After her blog brought me into a new world of online eating disorder kids, I gained tips … big tips … tips that I still use to this day – tips such as eating a "marker" (a brightly coloured food) first when binging so you didn't stop when you made yourself sick until you hit that colour … or how to run the shower or tap so no one heard you … or keeping a small bottle of cheap perfume on you at all times to cover the smell … or different hand techniques to hit your gag spot better … or how to move your fingers without choking yourself … or how to pull your hand away fast enough not to get sick on it. I could go on, but the best tip of all was … a hair tie. I always kept one on my left wrist, and it went up and down from my hair to my hand as frequently as a rollercoaster spins an adrenalin junkie at an amusement park. I think I always went for the left hand because what I was doing was anything but right.

For the next four years, I cruised those hallways. At school, we always had to have our hair up, but every now and then, I'd notice a girl with an extra hair tie on her left wrist. I'd wonder if maybe – just maybe – she was keeping this secret too.

Every bully has a diversion tactic.

She was no different.

You know how in primary school the playground bully never got in trouble? The bullies never got detention. Instead, it was the slightly less sneaky child who was just purely in the wrong place at the wrong time or who was bribed by a higher source with unlimited spaghetti toasties from the tuck shop if they took the fall – a scape goat.

Just like any other great manipulator, my bully was no different. And her target of choice? Food. Yup, good old yummy food … a key focal feature of life … the basis for enjoying life and for both strength and health. Some people think food is to blame for eating disorders. Wrong – food is food. It's designed to create pleasure, it's designed to be eaten in moderation, and it comes in a variety of types. If food was the cause of eating disorders, then maybe we'd all be at the back of a Boeing 707, doing what I was doing. But we aren't … well, I doubt *you* are, but I was. And all I thought was that this whole problem lay on the shoulders of Ben & Jerry's, Hershey's, Cadbury, and McDonald's *their CEOs are shaking*.

To my surprise, it was not the creation of McFlurries and fried chicken that meant I couldn't keep a single piece of food down for longer than 30 minutes. Rather, it was my *perception* of what those foods were doing to me that had me heaving. As soon as it hit my tongue, I felt an unbelievable urge to continuously eat as much of it as I physically could, and I mean literally shoveling food into me. It wasn't about enjoying it, it wasn't about needing it, and it wasn't about craving it. This was purely a quantity thing, and by about half-way through, everything tasted the same anyway, and I didn't even want it.

I felt targeted and cursed. I would walk into the supermarket, and all the wrappers would open their eyes, waiting to pounce on me. It felt unfair – really, really, really unfair. I formed a pure and utter hatred for food – all of it – including vegetables, meats, sweets, bread, milk, and cheese – anything and everything. I saw it as a numbers game. I remember sitting on my bed and explaining to my mum how much I hated food. I told her it made me fat and hideous, and when I ate it, it stuck to me. I could feel every piece go down my throat and land somewhere. I told her how it gave me cellulite, stretch marks, and acne.

Unfortunately for me, my fifteen-year-old awkward stage brought me all of that anyway, and I couldn't quite peg all the blame on nutrition. Regardless, I declared war – yup, a war bigger than both World Wars. They had nothing on me and my declared nemesis – nutrition. That scape goat we talked about earlier? Well, this was her plan the whole time, and whilst I would love to tell you the story of a girl and her body and her need to control it, this was so much more than that.

Bulimia was a diversion tactic for the badge I'd worn on my collar since I slid out of the womb. It was the blister on the back of my feet ... the prickling in my toes ... the scrape on my knee ... and the ache in my back. Bulimia took all the blame for her big sister – *Anxiety*. The solid truth is that I ate to push her down. I ate to suffocate her. I vomited to force her out. When she got loud, I tried to shut her up ... to get rid of her. She was Queen and the only ruler of my mind, spirit, and body.

I'd stared at plenty of walls in the offices of school counsellors and doctors, and I even found myself in a clairvoyant's bedroom when I was nineteen. Desperate for any cure that the pills weren't providing me. I went to a clairvoyant to talk to the other side, specifically my Grandma who'd passed away when I was younger. The experience was successful, and to this day, I remember what my Oma told me. She told me that I should stop hating myself because there are many people who wanted what I have or what I look like. I just couldn't see it.

She told me I couldn't hate myself happy.

She was right.

Toothbrush

I looked up to see the sign "toiletries" and took a sharp left. I was listening to a podcast from back home. I've always loved the New Zealand radio hosts so much more than the British ones. This week, I'd played about 20 of their podcasts back-to-back because hearing people talk all the time meant their voices would block out the ones in my head. It was a bad day, and she was yelling at me. She was telling me that he'd left me because the other girl was skinnier, prettier, and her thighs were more delicate. I knew it was true. That's the problem with her – she's not always wrong. He *had* left me. If only she'd left with him, maybe they could have gone on holiday to a "We-Like-to-Hurt-Cass" villa in the south of France.

I looked at the toothbrushes, obviously not the electric ones (ouch). I needed something big, but not too big … long, but not too long … one with no bumps, only a slight curve, and no change in texture. I needed something simple, and I found the winner – a half-clear/half-purple disposable generic toothbrush. My chosen weapon of mass destruction … the armour I wore to battle with myself … possibly the only thing I ever bought and used completely different to its intended purpose. You see, the bristles never touched my teeth. Instead, the handle slid straight down my throat. It was a tactic that only had success due to its unforgiving and constant push that was easily enhanced if needed.

She didn't stand a chance.

Food is a more than a taste. Food is a social thing. Food takes time. Food is compassion. Food is care. Food is creative. Food is comfort. Food reminds us of home. Food is a form of love.

That is why I got rid of it … because I didn't believe I deserved that. In a game of cat and mouse, I gave myself a taste of love, and then took it away.

I felt unworthy,
I still feel unworthy.

BULLY

I thought she was kind.
She was always there for me —
even at my lowest.
Late at night
when everyone was asleep,
I would get out of bed
she would come out of the closet.
She was the friend that held my hair,
rubbed my back,
rested her hand
on my shoulder.
She bent down
her hair brushed my check
she whispered,
"Keep going."

She was not kind
but she was persuasive,
encouraging.

I did what she said.
Until this day,
I have kept going.

"I heard you making yourself sick."

My heart stopped and so did her face because I couldn't lie to get away with this one. She was right – I had been making myself sick. I don't know why I did it, but I know it made me feel better – not afterwards though, only during the time. I've never admitted that until now, but it's true. It makes me feel less alone in a world where I have always been lonely. Like when he wouldn't text me back, and I would think he didn't care and say, "Fuck it!" and binge on $40 worth of food that I didn't even want. I never wanted this, but I chose it. Maybe I need to be more honest with myself and tell myself, *"I've heard you making yourself sick,"* because I had heard myself.

I've turned deaf to my own thoughts.

To lose touch with myself I put plastic against my skin. Wrapped measuring tapes around my waist, twisted my fingers around my wrists, held onto my collarbones with both hands, and dehydrated my lips. I stood with my feet on two different types of scales. I believed success was only valid in numbers.

I wasn't going to stop until

I was in first place.

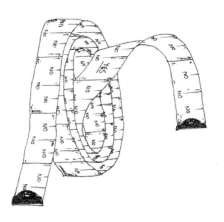

They only noticed me when there was less of me to notice.

She'll never leave. Don't pity me when you hear me say that because it's okay – I'm okay, and we're okay. We have a different relationship now. I tell her everything. I tell her when it's going well – when I have a good day and my heart is smiling. I also tell her when I'm heavy – when my thoughts are revolving like a pinwheel of doubt. It is not until I stop telling her things and start showing her my emptiness that she steps forward. She holds onto me, but not always tightly. I mean sometimes she suffocates me between her arms, but other times, she just kisses my ear – either way, I always know she is always there.

That is the comfort of an eating disorder. It is a terrible habit that is out of your control,

but it keeps you company.

BULLY

Is the space between you
and the girl next to you small?

Is your group of friends intimate?

Is that why I don't fit in?

Is that why I stand out?

Am I too big?

If I shrink, will you include me?

I was once told that there are three things that never stay hidden for long – the sun, the moon, and the truth.

My friends found me, my mum found me, my flatmates found me, and I found myself running low on excuses. There are only so many times you can blame food poisoning, alcohol, medication, or sickness for being caught with your head down a toilet. There are only so many times you can explain why you have two toothbrushes and often keep them in separate locations … why one is in your handbag … why you're always carrying tissues and taking Panadol … or why you're buying two of every chocolate bar in the confectionary isle. Me, myself, and I had to face what we were doing and that what we were doing was single-handedly destroying every form of normal behaviour. I suffered with constant issues with my skin, energy levels, and immune system. I developed health anxiety which would cause me to create symptoms that I didn't really have such as an irregular heartbeat or stabbing pain in my side.

All of this was occurring for the same reason that I couldn't order at a café without pre-planning what I was going to say ten times over … the same reason I wasn't able to go into shops and talk to assistants … the same reason I would cry for two hours before any party … the same reason I wasn't able to cross the road at certain crossings … why I never looked anyone in the eye … why I was constantly lying. This was occurring for the simple reason that I was doubting myself – all day, every day. Other kids grew up scared that something was in their closet, but my mind was a closet full of monsters with the light always out. I couldn't escape myself. I couldn't ignore myself, and I couldn't shake the message playing on repeat. It was like an old movie theatre projector constantly telling me,

"You're not good enough, and you never will be."

The following is how I proved that voice wrong ...

When I was 19, I went to a tattoo studio with one of my best friends. She told me that she'd booked an appointment with a guy who was really good – you know, one of those word-of-mouth recommendations (which is really what you want when getting someone to shove a needle into you). She'd gotten a time and was getting something for her grandma, and to my luck, she offered me a window of opportunity to tag along (and also maybe get my skin scratched). Let's keep in mind that this information came into my life approximately 24 hours before I found myself pulling my jeans down in front of a decently attractive male in his early thirties with a full sleeve and a septum piercing. Just like every other teenager-about-to-become-young-adult, I had a few ideas of tattoos I liked, but I'd never found anything I could commit to.

With a peppermint tea in hand the night before, I hit a quote like no other quote I'd ever found. Pinterest was my safe haven for overly emotional writing about ex-boyfriends, and therefore, it was a place I spent a lot of my spare time. But never in my copious hours of scrolling had I seen a sentence like this one. When I saw it, I didn't even need to read it twice to know I wanted to read it every day for the rest of forever. Maybe, dear reader, you've never seen it before, so this one's for you. I hope you love it as much as I do – and I love it so much I've got it tattooed on my ass!

You are enough.

When I read this, I remember that wherever I am right now – no matter what weight, what grades I've gotten, what relationship I'm in, what job I'm working, or what I'm doing every day – it is totally 100% ideal and more than good enough. It's amazing! It makes me realize that I am exactly where I need to be. Just like a map at the zoo marked with "You Are Here", I am in the right place.

You are not reading this by accident. Everything I just said applies to you too, and I want you to know how unbelievably good enough for life you truly are.

When he walked out on me, *she* threw her arms up in celebration. She had always detested the idea of sharing. She was one of those possessive friends – the ones who don't let you hang out with anyone else. Her loving strokes of my hair made me feel like I didn't need anyone else. She made me feel wanted, and I hated that she could do that. She still holds my hand, but now instead of trying to push her away, I talk to her. I tell her that there are other things that make me feel wanted too … that my comfort doesn't just come from her … that I can have other habits aside from heaving myself over toilets and spending too long in the confectionary aisle of supermarkets. In her defence, she's been a good friend but also a fantastic bully – a wonderful oxymoron, and I admire her power. I wish I was that powerful … maybe I am because I kind of created her. Maybe she's me – superhero me – with the ability to capture and persuade even the most protected of hearts.

Maybe that's the key to recovery … maybe that's what nobody tells you … how powerful you are – so powerful you can control yourself to the highest degree. Maybe she's the best thing that ever happened to you, and maybe you're stronger than you think.

TO DO LIST

She gives me a to-do list every day, starting with overthinking and prioritizing doubt then ending in depression. She tells me her way is the only way, and at the end of the day, she sits at the end of my bed and gives me an analysis on what I did wrong and how I could have done things differently. She tells me how it was all unsatisfactory – even down to how I chewed my food and started my car. I know she tells you the same things too. Sometimes you can hear her over the people speaking to you. I know she is distracting. She tells you not to tell anyone because she is not the problem – you are. She tells you they won't understand anyway. If she was a person, you'd block her on social media and maybe move schools or friendship groups. How do you block your own mind? How do you move away from your head? Is that why you always try to run away? Is that why you can't commit to anything?

Dear runaway girl, this is your guide to facing commitment. You only fear attachment because you have been emotionally, mentally, and physically attached to the wrong things. You've been attached to her. You are not committed to being caged. Stop thinking about her as hard matter. She is not made of metal bars or barbed wire. She is not solid. This is not a curse, and it does not have to continue. She is lying to you; misleading you. You're going to be okay, and you do not have to complete the checklist of worries she whispers in your ear. You can ignore them. Fail her tasks. You can prove her wrong.

BULLY

She will try to handcuff you,
but she is not the authority —
you are.

Lock her up.

How do I stop the voice in my head?

Stop talking to yourself.

Maybe if we selected our thoughts as carefully as the photos we post on Instagram, we wouldn't have this problem.

I ran into an old friend.

I could still recognise her, even though her back was facing me. It didn't really matter anyway because I couldn't remember what her face looked like. It was a face that changed a lot, you see. Sometimes she smiled, but sometimes her teeth doubled in size, with fangs handing out either side, and eyes rotating until they were blood-red.

She reminded me of a light switch. She would be beautiful, and then – flick – she would look like she was going to eat me alive.

In the past, I let her eat me alive.

She was a weird friend.

I don't really know how to explain it to you, but she had this ability to make me feel like the most important person in the world. She'd love me, support me, and always be by my side, gently rubbing my back or holding my hand. Then she would just dump me into a situation and leave me hanging with no life jacket on – alone, isolated, and unsure. You know when you have a comfort? Maybe a comfort person, food, space, blanket, etc., and then it leaves, and you feel even more uncomfortable than before they were even there? Well, that was her. She was always by my side.

But she played games.

This time, I stood beside her. I thought about the pros and the cons and everything in between, and I decided she was more trouble than good. I didn't have time to fall down a vortex, so I decided to pretend I hadn't seen her. Like thirteen-year-old me avoiding my crush, I quickly walked past her. I kept my head down and didn't look up. I pretended to be on my phone, answering an anonymous call. I walked quickly as fast as I could, and then I ran. Truth be told, I was scared of her, and I didn't need or want to live scared anymore. But I was scared now. I was scared of being scared – her ultimate goal.

A flashing red light ahead brought me to a stop. Out of breath and with a sense of both relief and terror, I checked behind me to see if she was catching up, but she wasn't there.

The light turned green, and I took a huge stride to re-enter my run – re-enter my fear of fear – and as my foot hit the concrete and my head spun toward the direction I was going, I slammed into her. Full speed. My whole body pressed against hers like I was hitting the hardest ten-foot-high brick wall. That was it – that's how I always found her.

I hit the wall.

I ran into an old friend today.

This time I hit her so hard that I felt every piece of my soul shatter into smithereens around me. Every piece of me burst open so wide that I gulped for air, thinking about how I'd never get everything back together ever again. It was as I looked at my world in pieces that I felt her gentle warmth on my arm, on my back, and holding my hand, and I could feel her smiling. She was reminding me that she'd always be there. This was her plan all along – to break me and then watch me have to put myself back together again.

My old friend. How many times have we done this?
My old friend, I have something to confess to you. Now that I am older, wiser, and taller, I am also smarter and with this comes skills – skills you haven't seen. In a weird way, I have missed your comfort. But I have not missed the sleepless nights, and I cannot continue this relationship anymore.

I know you love watching me scatter, but this time – this time I will show you how I can put the jigsaw puzzle back together. I can put it back together faster, better, and stronger than ever before.
I ran into an old friend – yup, literally. And guess what? It was destructive and brutal, and I couldn't breathe.

But the joke is that although I may be her Rubik's cube, I'll make sure that this time, she will never, ever, ever figure me out.

Not ever, ever, ever again.

To begin recovery,
you must only change one thing –
your mind.

It does not matter if I slip up, fuck up, or mess up. It does not matter if I am not fully healed because I accept that I will never be fully healed. What matters most is that I stand up for myself against my own mind. What matters most is that I am on my way. What matters most is that I am learning to break bad habits, and that I have stopped licking the open wound you left me with while still expecting it to heal.

It tends to be the invisible things that are actually the most blinding.

– Mental illness.

Healing is a trip without a map. There is no end, no destination and you do not know what exit you are meant to take what road to turn down. It is trial and error. U-turns, dead-ends, and speed bumps are inevitable.

You will never arrive,
but keep going.

A letter to myself on days when it gets to hard:

Drop the rules you shackle yourself to. Take a deep breath. You are trying so hard to over-perform that you can't see how badly you are over-doing it.

I know you hide everything that's wrong, but you can't live your life hiding. If you keep it up, these hidden things will eventually explode – just like you have.

Please, let it all out. Let yourself feel it. And when your soul collapses and you don't think you can keep going and the pressure you have been under forms the tears in your eyes that run down your cheeks, know that this is not weakness.

This is strength.
You have been carrying the world for too long – no wonder it's getting heavy. Don't feel pathetic. Feel proud that you have made it this far, and you can make it through this too.

My dear perfectionist,
you do not need to always get it right.

You kill them with kindness whilst killing yourself with comparison.

People always ask me what having anxiety disorder feels like, and I often describe it like this … In a car park, roughly 99% of the cars are totally normal. When they get locked up, the alarm only goes off if the car is being broken into. However, we've all seen that one car when maybe the wind blew too strong, the trees rustled too loudly, or someone walked past too close, and for no obvious reason, the alarm goes off. You walk past and look at it, and it just sits there with its screaming signal for no fucking point. *Well, that's me.*

My Mum and I had an interesting conversation after we watched a movie recently. It was a thriller, and while she was very scared by it, I wasn't scared at all. She asked me how I'd survived all the "frights" in the film. You see, after studying film for three years, I'm pretty well-versed about the direction and production of these things. I explained how anticipation is built into films in order to create the jump, climax, or plot twist. I told her how certain shots, angles, sounds, and dialogues are used in order to build a specific feeling in the viewer. It can start building up to three scenes before the climactic scene.

"It's not just about what you're looking at; it's how you're being made to look at it."

"Cass, if you are able to analyse how a director is making you feel anxious in a film, how does that help you analyse what makes you feel anxious in life?"

I was still caught up in that question a few hours later. I used to think anxiety was this really big thing – like a huge stack of bricks that I balanced on my back every day. I was wrong. Anxiety is being paralysed over the fear of dropping just a single brick and the pressure I put on myself to balance it, not the stack itself. Anxiety is small ... actually, it's really tiny. It's a single stomach flip, one heavier heartbeat. It's the panic over a dropped coin. It's the short breaths. It's an opened message. It's thinking a sentence through three times before you speak. It's looking at the ground because you can't make eye contact. It's cancelled plans. It's fiddling your fingers. It's bitten nails, and it's spilling your coffee because of your shaking hands. *It's doubting yourself on every turn, every decision, every second.* And yes, that is big, but what makes it big are the little things that add up. Just like in the movies, it's not the situation that's happening. It's HOW it's happening that makes you feel anxious. If you struggle with anxiety, be aware of the little things. That person you think is looking at you weird – it's probably just their face. No – you didn't say the wrong thing. Yes – it's okay that you sit at home in tears instead of going out. Instead of panicking over balancing those bricks, let them drop off your back. Let them fall. Let the car alarm go off. Stop anticipating the outcome of a situation, and just let yourself get a fright. Love the uncertainty.

When you stop trying to control the little things, the big picture suddenly won't seem so heavy.

I promise.

Social Anxiety

Friday nights were for my friends to sip mixed drinks at room temperature, my acquaintances to smoke on the couch, and for all of them to laugh. You see, they all had an inside joke that I wasn't included in. It must have been some simultaneously serious, hilarious, informative, and personal thing that meant they all had something in common. Perhaps it was their lack of fear. I, however, was not in on the joke. And by not being in on the joke, I truly realised that I was as different as I felt. Being a wallflower is one thing, and for me, it didn't happen naturally. Instead, I made a conscious effort.

Whenever I felt myself floating away, I threw on my invisibility cloak. All it took to put it on was the split decision in which I made up my mind to evaporate into thin air, and with that, it would wrap me around into nothingness. This is how I learned about people – by being a self-made fly on the wall. Their voices were clear and unmistakable. They didn't ask where I had gone or why I had left because I never truly left. I could probably tell you more about them than they could about themselves. That's the thing with invisibility, you get to know people even though they can't see you.

They never saw me, and that is because I didn't want them to.

Depression.

My fingers tightened around the wooden handle. I'm not sure why theme parks always make me nervous, but I guess being nervous and being excited is kind of the same thing, just like thrill and fear are intertwined. I licked the candy floss that was hanging from my outer lip, flinging my body to the side as a clown car went screaming past me. Beside me, one of the bigger rollercoasters looped around with faint screams, but my gaze was set on the best ride of all — the Ferris wheel.

The Ferris wheel always had a long line, but it was always worth the wait. You went all the way to the top and back down — around and around, never ending. It was simultaneously consistent and inconsistent. You knew what was going to happen, but you always got frightened at the top. I got to the front of the queue and saw the glowing sign — Depression. I was in the right place and ready for my turn. I stepped onto the swinging carriage, sitting down on the well-worn leather seat. The doors closed behind me as the world went numb. The sounds became muffled, but I could still hear the tinkling of music in the background. We climbed all the way up, and I noticed that I was not the only one riding alone. For some reason, we were all sitting in our own carriages. No one was in pairs.

It was a lonely ride, even though you knew other people were on it too. With two loud clanks, my carriage arrived at the top, and I looked out at the theme park of my mind. Elephants bowed in the background, and bumper cars slammed into each other. It was chaos, but a warm and welcoming chaos. As you could have guessed, it was at the top where I got terrified and held my breath. My hands went white, and it felt like we would never return to the ground. "Maybe I should jump out?" I said to myself. My hair was stuck to the back of my neck with sweat, and my vision was starting to blur. As everything began to feel like too much, that's when I heard it – the thud of the wheel starting again to bring me back down and send someone else to the top. The carriage swayed in the wind and made its way down toward the end slowly. Around and around and around she spun.

To all dear girls (including myself) – your own opinion about your physical appearance should *not* be defined by the following:

1. Numbers on a scale
2. Instagram models
3. Size labels on clothing
4. Your cup size
5. When your jeans feel tight after being washed
6. The piece of birthday cake you ate last week
7. The number of likes on a photo
8. Your friends' bodies
9. Genetics
10. The girl sitting next to you
11. Opinions
12. The way women are talked about in the media
13. The way women are talked about in music
14. The rip in your over-worn leggings
15. Cm's, mm's, or inches
16. The boy who told you to lose weight
17. Your favourite meal out
18. The widest point of your hips
19. Eating a block of chocolate when you get your period
20. The amount of make-up you wear
21. How far you can run
22. Your boyfriend's ex
23. Any man's opinion. Full. Stop.
24. Your own self-criticism

Your thoughts are not legally binding documents. You are not required to do as they say – they are negotiable and optional. You can fight them back. Your thoughts can tell you off as many times as they want, but that does not mean you have to do what they say.

Do you realise that by comparing yourself to your friend all night, you are letting the fact that she has a 63cm waist when you have a 67cm waist ruin how you're experiencing life? You're letting 4 cm stop you from going on an adventure.

Numbers are measurements – they are not restrictions.

Growth isn't easy.
Why do you think they call them *growing pains?*

Your anxiety is playing the same movie in your head but rewriting the script each night. It is trying to tell you what could have happened if you'd just made a different decision, done something more, tried harder, or been lighter. This movie is getting old, and the options are getting limited. Tell your anxiety that people come and go regardless of who is in the closing scene. You've got to stop directing this movie. It's keeping you awake.

Just roll the credits.

I have loved everything with all my heart, and nothing has ever loved me back as much as I loved it. That is why I have always been heartbroken – not by other people, but by myself because I've given people my all without any litmus test of their intentions. And thus, I have fallen from terrible heights. When you fall, you break. When things break, they get rebuilt. I have used my ability to love to my advantage because I turned it inwards. I stuck my broken pieces from loving other people back together by loving myself, and that is why I am strong. It is because I have known what it is like to be weak.

It was a bright thought. Light, yet still poignant. It was in the very centre of my mind. It was not overwhelming. It was bright, but it wasn't blinding. It just sort of felt ... natural. Yeah, I guess "natural" is a word that you're probably thinking shouldn't be such an alarming thing, right? Well, hang on – let me tell you the thought. I lay there, covered in sweat with my back pressed flat against my yoga mat, my feet together, and my knees open in some sort of relaxed fish pose. Suddenly I thought,

"God, I love you!"

It was from my brain to my body ... like one of those stickers your mum puts on your Christmas present – "To: Body. Merry Christmas! From: Brain". Now, I know you're thinking I'm fucking crazy, and first of all, that's true. But stay with me. This was the first time in my entire life that my brain had voluntarily told my body that I loved it. In the past, my mind, conscience, and soul had mumbled kind words to me and my physical appearance when targeted or held at gun-point to do so, but this was different. This just came from nowhere. It was like a U.F.O. – unexpected and foreign. I didn't know if I should believe it was real or not. But before I could process any of this, that bright bulb started to turn up the light. It was undeniable, and it was filling me up. My eyes were closed, and the sides of my mouth started to lift.

"I love you," I thought in wonderment and peace.

"I love your hips that rock when you walk and don't fit any pair of jeans well. I love your lower stomach fat, even though you bust your ass in the gym and eat healthy. I love your broad shoulders. I love your acne scars. I love your left tit (significantly smaller than the right one). But even more so, I love that you have carried me this far, through it all. You've supported me even just through this. It's been me and you, and you always had my back. I love you."

It was speaking, just plain speaking. It wasn't yelling, and it didn't sound persuasive. It just sounded honest. I'd never had a thought like this before, but I liked it. I welcomed it. I would have liked to make it tea and tell it to take a seat. I was unsure how to keep it in my head, but I didn't want to cage it. I just wanted to enjoy it. I kept it there, soft and steady. I thought about how I would not be sad when it left because I knew another would come.

Many poems and people will try and tell you what self-love is. But when you tell your own self that you're in love with you, then maybe you're on the right track. Earlier in that yoga class, we were working at aligning our posture, beginning in downward dog with one leg lifted. We were then asked to raise our hand in order to grab the ankle of the foot on the ground – a serious balancing act. We all fell, and the yoga teacher said, "That's the brilliance of it. For a few seconds, all that existed in your brain was your hand touching your ankle."

She was right.

That was brilliant and very hard. It took me 21 years, a lot of toilets, a lot of toothbrushes, a lot of long showers, a lot of doubt, and a lot of mean thoughts to realise that self-love was something that needed to exist entirely in my brain, even for a few seconds.

All I needed to do was grab my ankle.

My Body

Through the heartbreaks and losses of my life, I have always wondered what it would be like to be able to forgive. Like a fake laugh, I smeared forgiveness across my face, hiding my rage behind it. But all this time, my mind was not aware of how you forgave me. After everything I've done to you … every toilet you've heaved over at the will of the fingers I forced into your throat … every meal you've skipped … every night you've starved … every workout that lasted one or three hours too long … every pill I made you process to help my mind lose control … after all of that, you forgave me. I break my arms, you heal. I damage my ankle, you rebuild. I get sick, you get better. Without hesitation, you help me. After everything I've done to you, you continue to help me. I searched to find an example of forgiveness across the world, when the example was right before me – it was you.

I wrote about you and I.

Calm down, it's not a love letter. Love letters do not have titles, and this has a title. This has a title because you and I never did. Bittersweet. That's you, my darling, everything good and everything poisonous all at once, just how I like it. I did not write this for you. I wrote this for my future daughter. When she is crying herself to sleep over the wrong boy with a fast car, I will have something to show her … something to explain to her how it will all make sense someday …. something for when he leaves her, so I will be able to tell her that boys are harder to get rid of than one's 17-year-old self might expect.

This is everything we were and everything we were not…

Part Two

EVERYTHING
I WANTED TO SAY
BUT DIDN'T

I have treated you as if you were the cure, when in reality, you have always been the curse.

It was not the final bow, the crowd's applause, the closed curtains, or the ending which hurt the most. It was that we could have been the most spectacular show on earth, yet we never made it past rehearsals.

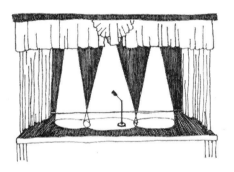

It only took three words to make a writer speechless.

"I love you."

I was choking on sentences, punctuation and prose. Unsure of which words to spit out. I didn't know if I could repeat the same sentiment back to you. It didn't feel right. A war between my brain and my heart ignited. My mind wanted to know if you were sure about this … to ask you why? Why now? My brain needed answers, and she wanted you to know that you were two years too late. Then the small voice of my heart whispered gently … she sighed "finally." She asked me to tell you how long she has waited to hear that as she is still sitting on the front steps, expecting your car to pull into the driveway. The broken brain and the hopeful heart went to war. Your slip-ups and trip-ups and unfulfilled promises replayed in my mind, but so did the good times. I wanted good times more than I wanted to remember the reality – the reality that the good times were not that good because I remembered them how I wanted to remember them. I remembered that you were loyal, when in fact, you were anything but that.

Instead of the brain and the heart, in the end, it was my soul who spoke.

The innermost me rose from her resting place within my bones.

She stood up and said, "I love**d** you too."

My sanity swings like a pendant around your neck.

BULLY

I took off my rose-tinted glasses and saw you for what you really were – black and white.

Our relationship reminds me of a tight rope –
unstable, unpredictable, unstructured, risky, and used
for entertainment. I step on it, knowing the
challenge ahead... knowing I have failed in the past...
knowing that I will inevitably fall off, and yet still
holding onto the hope that I'll make it to the other
side.

The balancing act continues.

Please stop shaking the rope.

You confessed your love to my hips before you said it to my face. Perhaps that was the first warning sign that you were going to build a holiday home out of me because you sought your escapism based on the design of the place and not the interior.

BULLY

You are trespassing.
Get off the grass.
Climb back over the fence.
The alarm is going off.
The dog will get you.
Do not enter where you are not welcome.
Read the sign I put up.
You are banned.
Keep out.

Take twice a day with food – betrayal. Swallow this with 40ml of your insecurities and feel your insides bubble. This is a prescribed course of antibiotics to help fight the infection of deception that you seem to be struggling with. This is my revenge. You are not a qualified practitioner, yet my affection for you awarded you a certificate of trust – a trust which lead me to accept whatever you placed in the palm of your hand and extended to me. Now I refuse to take your pills. They have not helped me; they have made me crazy. You have inserted needles into me … dripped syrups into my bloodstream to numb my mind from your actions. You dulled my nervous system to override my anxiety-ridden brain. My most marvellous tool of overthinking, which possibly could have thought of something to save me sooner. Spray this in the back of your throat to swallow the reality of your decisions and suck on the consequences of your behaviour. Sour, isn't it? Bitter? Yes, lying leaves a bad taste in your mouth, doesn't it?

A taste of your own medicine.

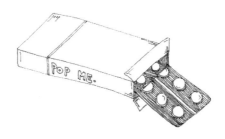

BULLY

We built a home together, but little did we know we were only making sandcastles. As soon as the tide came in, we washed away.

You stabbed me in my back, but you brought a knife to a gun fight, and I shot down our love.

— *You're not the only bad guy here.*

BULLY

When you're in...
the back of a lecture chewing on a pencil,
on a bus gazing out a window,
driving the same route you always take to the gym,
listening to music on your lunch break,
or alone and drunk in the bathroom at a party.
When you're daydreaming,
asleep,
in the middle of a nightmare –

when your mind leaves your body,
I hope it visits me.

I am not the solution to your loneliness.

BULLY

The gods cried out
on the night they first saw it.

My flash light
swinging around in the dark,
looking for you.
Their pity forked
in knives of
lightning.

They knew
I'd lose you one day.

Love is blind, yet I consistently wore a reflective vest, praying you'd notice me first.

I hope you have fun with the girls injected with nonsense. I hope you talk to them, and they have nothing to say. I hope you remember how we'd get interrupted from our sentence to the sun rising because we couldn't shut up. I hope they get up out of your bed and leave you and you remember my fingers tracing your side at 3 a.m. I hope you sit there staring at your designer clothes and miss seeing mine scattered across your bedroom floor. I hope you get every inch of luxury, fame, money, and success, and when you get it all, I hope you call me to tell me that none of it will ever be as valuable as what you and I had. And when you call me, I hope I'll be far away – in the land of the meaningful where I have always lived my life and where you have never bothered to visit.

When our time was running out, I kept making my hips roll anti-clockwise. I tried to stop the hands from shifting by keeping yours on me. The right direction was never straightforward, but we didn't know how actually t o move forward.

We were always better at going in circles.

I am paranoid that the sky will fall without you beside me, so I will keep staring at your ceiling long after I should have left in order to avoid it caving in.

Did you take a hammer to my heart so you could
always have a piece of it?

I have missed calls from you because you've been looking for me behind the eyes of other girls again.

You won't find me there.

BULLY

I don't believe you.
Your mouth is saying one thing,
but your eyes are telling me another.
Your words seem polished.
Have you practiced them before?
Have you sorted and organized them?
Colour coded them?

Did you use them on her?
Did she fall for them too?

I will never apologize for leaving as it took you seeing another man love me to realise I was worthy of loving.

But, I am even more sorry that I didn't feel worthy of love until I let another man love me.

Loving you was like paper mache. It was taking care to pull apart shreds of the different versions of you, that you gave me. It was sticking them together to make something whole. Piece by piece. It was creative, it was art, and it was difficult. It required skill, time and attention to detail - not just anyone could do it.

It was using extra glue on the thinner strips to hold them together and to make sure they didn't rip. It was taking paper and asking it to no longer be flexible, to transform out of its purpose, to be unreadable and to make a new shape.

It was unnatural.

If you love me as much as you say you do, then why do you continue to hurt me? I'm not blind. I see how you look at other girls when you think my back is turned to you. You look at them like a crocodile looks at a lamb - with an intention. You look at girls like you're looking at meat.

You capture empty hearts, drag them into your room, and confuse their souls with soft touches. You take what you want from them.

What you don't realise is that when you do this, you're also taking a piece of my trust, placing it on a wooden chopping board, and slashing it in half with a butcher's knife. As your hands slip deeper and deeper up her thighs, you sink my confidence lower and lower. Each kiss you plant on her stomach is a cigarette burn in my back.

You make me ask myself what I'm doing wrong when you are the one abusing my trust. You make me doubt myself. Hate myself. You disappear into her arms and come home to me three days later. You don't love me – you never did. You only love that I stroke your ego, moan your name, kiss your neck, and tell you that you are my king.

My body is no longer your kingdom. This is not your place to rule. You are no longer in control.

I'm closing the gates to this castle.

You treat women like lollipops – suck them until they run out of flavour.

BULLY

Everything happens for a reason, but I am wondering what reason is there for my constant need to wear your shirt before I go to bed in order to feel encompassed by you? Why do I want to feel consumed? Why do I drink a glass of wine and my tongue traces the letters of your name on the inside of my teeth? Why do the songs we listened to play in cars and bars? Why does my body feel happiest when your hands are on it?

If everything happens for a reason, then tell me what reason there is for you not being here right now. Tell me what I did right to deserve you.

Tell me the reason why I miss you and tell me the reason why I have no idea if you still miss me.

You hadn't tried drugs before I met you, and maybe that's why you liked me. Even without substances, you found a way to get high.

Is that why you've started smoking now that I'm gone?

You told me you would give me the world. It was surprising to find that you'd taped it into sections. You must have told her you would give her the same thing. I guess it is a very big place, and we can share. She can have the rainforest, and I can have the Pacific Ocean. She can have London, and I'll take Los Angeles. She can claim the pyramids, but I will take Mount Everest.

She can have your body, and I will hold your heart.

When the one who got away comes home, do you open the front door? I know he's toxic, but he's knocking. Is it rude not to respond? Now he's kicking, banging, and yelling at the door. You have spent so long building up these walls – does he deserve to step inside them again? When logic and love create two different opinions in your mind, it is fucking suffocating. You feel trapped.

When this happened to me, I turned to the greats. I read Hemingway, Bronte, and Austin. I analysed Banksy, Van Gough, and Monet. I listened to Houston, Winehouse, and Sinatra. I watched Hitchcock, Tarantino, and Anderson. What did they have for me? The books, the art, the songs, the films – surely the loves and lives that legends had would answer some of my questions. But they returned with nothing, and I was still empty-handed.

I began to beg the solar system to make this work. I begged for the key to open the door to him, but the stars were straight-faced, the planets were asleep, the sun was unimpressed, and the universe is always stubborn. I found no answer in what to do.

It was when I turned my question inwards that I found an answer right in front of me. The heart and the brain don't often disagree, but when they do, listen to your stomach. The vessel that was once filled with butterflies was now retracting with fear. The stomach remembers the lessons of the past more so than the brain or the heart. For the stomach has heaved and cried and processed the wine and drugs you took to silence the brain and numb the heart.

So finally, after exhausting every exterior source, I asked my body for the key. I was surprised when it spoke, for it told me to open my eyes and realise that I had built walls to keep something out ... to keep safe ... to keep pain out. I had built a bunker of sorts. I built walls to survive ... I built walls to keep you away.

It is my fault that I confused these walls for shelter. These walls are not a home, and I am not confined to them or to the insecurities you made me live with. With no barrier up or holding me in, there was only one thing left to do ...

Move forward.

I'm sorry I couldn't let you in.

To you, I was an appetizer. You chewed my soul, swallowed my body, stood up, and ordered another girl for the main course.

"I don't know — I don't know why one person can impact you so much. To everyone else, your relationship makes no sense. But to you, the sun rises every morning and says, "Thank God for _____.""

"Who does your sun rise for, Cass?"

A knock-back realisation. Your laugh rang in my ears, and the sound of the door closing behind you did too. I've stayed floating in a mirage of moving on, but moving and loving are just one letter apart. I loved you the entire time you were gone. Like a contortionist, I pretended to be over you … pretended like you were eradicated from my mind. I flipped lies. Like a professional, I just flipped myself in and out of cars, planes, and trains to try and run away from something I could never escape — my mind. Nevertheless, I continued … until one day I realised that even though I can numb the night with alcohol, questionable decisions, and bad dance moves, I can never avoid the morning after. Nothing is as clockwork as days, and the days end in nights, no matter what state you've got yourself in. I can say I've moved on, but the sun will keep rising. And for me, it will always say, "Thank God for _____." and I will keep loving you.

- Fill in the Blank

Give me all of it –
the ring,
the proposal,
you on your knees.
Cry.
Give me the flowers,
the ceremony,
our babies' first steps,
family dinners,
and the big car.
Our parents holding hands.
Give me your vows,
your promises,
your commitment.

You and I
have two options –

Everything or Nothing at all.

We are plastic, always recycling one another.

To impress you, I have exhausted myself, burdened myself, and ruined myself. I feel like a wet towel that has been rung out and squeezed of every drop inside me. I have bled myself dry for you, changed my mind for you, cut my hair, pierced my ear, and tried to look younger. I got tattoos — I hope you like them. I hope you like them more than I do. I tried to be interesting, I tried to read more books, and watch more films so I would have something to talk to you about. Maybe we don't actually have anything in common. Maybe that is why I tried to like the things that you like so we would have something in common. I hoped if I was talented, similar, and special that you would be impressed … that you would be interested in me … like I am interested in you. But maybe I'm not even interested … maybe I'm just obsessed. I'm obsessed with proving you wrong. I grew up admiring the big kids, the people who were entirely themselves. But now, now I have lost myself trying to impress someone who doesn't know who I really am … someone who I have now made sure, never will.

BULLY

My eyes blinked rapidly,
shifted my gaze under the sun.
Your name didn't pulse through my veins.
It didn't spill off my tongue every few seconds.
I hadn't thought about you in a while...
a day, if not days.
When I thought of you,
I couldn't quite feel you,
or see you as
clearly as I used to.
You were not a solid foundation in my brain,
but you were still there but
liquefied,
translucent,
like water
running through hands.

You were slipping from my mind.

I type texts and then delete them. I write poems and don't publish them. I practice speeches and don't say them. I don't know how to explain myself and I don't know if I should tell you...

tell you that I regret it.

I regret choosing him over you.

You are mistaking me for someone else. You do not want me back. How can you want me if you don't even know me? You only know her. The girl wearing low cut tops to impress you, sprinkling glitter on her collar bones and trying to make out with other guys to make you jealous. She was 17 and impressionable. She drank straight vodka with a smile… vodka she brought with a fake ID, but she told you her real name. She wore denim shorts and tripped over her untied shoelaces. She was a fantastic actor, appearing brave by dancing on tables, wearing too much make-up, and hanging out with any crowd of kids who were having fun. But let's be real, she was secretly shitting herself. She was smart, and I admire her for jumping in the deep end, but when it came to you she was stupid … really stupid. Being with you was stupid. Well, a stupid idea. I remember that version of you, the you with the longer hair, skinnier frame, faster walk, and wandering eye. I bet she's still out there, running around a concert that she doesn't have a ticket to, wearing your jacket, and texting her parents, convincing them that she's staying at a friend's house. So if you say you want me back, just know you are wrong – you want her. You can find her. I have no idea where she is, you see she's hard to track down. She has no moral compass. You will need to map out her mind and pinpoint her happy place. It shouldn't be too hard to do, considering her happy place… well you see…

it was always you.

I had flashbacks of us.
It looked like a kaleidoscope of love.
I shook the pieces
and saw that it was just
lust
disguised,
dressed up in pretty colours.

It wasn't real.
It was an
illusion -
just like
You.

You know that feeling you get – when your mum makes your favourite home-cooked dinner … when someone you work with remembers to ask you about the date you went on the other night … when your friend picks you up and drops you home … when you get into your bed that's just been made with fresh sheets … when your dog or cat rests their head on your knee … when the café up the road remembers your coffee order … when it's finally payday and you can buy the shoes you were saving for … when a stranger smiles at you on the street … when you get a better grade on a test than you expected … when someone compliments your skin … when you finish the last page of a book … when your favourite song comes on the radio … when your jeans aren't as tight on you as they were a month ago (even after a wash) … and when you re-read a Christmas card from someone you love?

This is the only way I could think of to explain how it felt when he came back.

Comfortable.

But what good has ever come from comfort zones?

You are heartless, but that doesn't matter because my heart is yours to keep anyway.

I wonder if it is raining where you are. It is raining here, and that reminds me of you. I wonder if it reminds you of me too. I wonder if you were thinking as carefully as I was on our last morning in bed together. I wonder if you were thinking of how the middle of my back felt under your fingers. I wonder if you said to yourself, "Remember this because I don't know when you're going to feel it again." I wonder if that scared you. I wonder if you're as scared as I am. I wonder if you felt it … if you felt your stomach drop as you stood on the edge and peered over into the darkness. I wonder if you know what I know. I wonder if you know what's going to happen. I wonder if you're ready to fall. I wonder if you remember how to use a parachute. I wonder if you even want to be saved … I wonder if you know that I don't. I wonder if you knew we were going to fall from the second you saw me. I wonder if I knew it then too.

I wonder if you're alone after a busy day and look at your toothbrush and remember mine next to it. I wonder if you still use my moisturiser and remember my hands.

I wonder if you miss me … if you miss me even half as much as I miss you?

BULLY

You grabbed my wrist,
pinned me against the wall and
screamed at me.
You told me I was an idiot to leave you,
that without you I would fail.
Fall
into depression –
emptiness.
That I would be unfulfilled.
Yes,
that would be terrible.
Those are terrible things,
but I would rather be all of them
instead of feeling how I felt when I was with you

– Alone.

All I wanted was for you to be happy and she was the only person who could make that happen.

So, I let her love you too.

Sacrifice.

Take care of him for me.

Getting caught without an umbrella in the rain.

Something that makes you half panic and half laugh – something unplanned, frustrating and yet absolutely perfect. Something that makes you run for cover. Something that you wish you had been warned about. Something you wish you could have predicted.

That was me and you.

Get busy – you've got an enormous task ahead of you as you need to taste every flavour of girl. On your journey, you'll meet some that are smart, funny, empty, ignorant, stylish, sexy, artistic, talented, messy, and all of them will not be me.

So go, go and have fun with those girls that you look at in the rear view mirror. Go and run your fingers over a girl who is drunk off alcohol you've paid for and wearing your jacket home even though you're cold. Go and take her clothes off and examine her skin. Only then will you realise she doesn't have the same sunspots as I do, her thighs don't wrap around you as tightly as mine do, and her teeth hit against yours when you kiss. Compare her, and I like a middle school science project. Create graphs about each of us.

Who is better? Who is prettier?

Then go and find another girl, then another one, and another. Wake up next to one that smells like burnt coffee and think about how I only drank decaffeinated cappuccinos. You will wake up to a cloud of perfume that you don't recognise and you'll think about how my hair smelt like salted caramel spread across your pillow, and only then will you remember you have a sweet tooth.

Go and explore until one day when your fingers stop hovering over my name, and they finally slip. Explore until the day comes that you get the urge to buy your ticket home.

You'll stand at my front door with an unzipped raincoat on and a spoon in your pocket. You'll tell me that they didn't taste like me, they didn't fit like me, and they didn't know you the same way that I know you. That they didn't understand you. You'll pause ... you'll drop to your knees ... you'll kiss my hand ... you'll tell me that I'm the one. I'll tell you that everyone has a favourite flavour, but it shouldn't have taken you this long to figure out what you like most ... I'll tell you time doesn't heal all wounds — sometimes time makes them thicker, hurt more, ooze puss, and re-open the stitches.

My cuts dripped blood while you dripped new flavours on your hands and licked them up your arm.

You'll taste every girl just to come back and tell me, "You're the best I've ever had."

And I'll reply, **"I know."**

BULLY

I wandered away down a new path,
unintentionally.
I simply followed a new voice.
His was deeper than yours.
I lost us and I found what I was looking for
– him.
But I am writing this to confess that
I still hold onto a secret hope
that my directions home
take me back to
you.

To forget me will be as simple as taking the blue from the sea, the clouds from the sky, the heat from the sun, the shine from the moon, the trees from the forests, the green from the grass, and the memories of my tongue from your mind.

Impossible.

Fuck you.

Fuck you. Fuck you for ruining love, feelings, and men for me. No, I am not referring to the fact that you have made sure that every time any guy shows interest in me, I will automatically assume that he has selfish intentions with me. No, I mean fuck you for treating me better than anyone ever has ... for showing me exactly what I want in someone and then taking it away at the snap of your fingers. Fuck you for taking the word "trust" out of my vocabulary because you put all your trust in me, and that finally made me feel worthy.

Now you're gone, and I feel useless. I am not sure what point I started to exist only for your reactions and responses, but all I know is that right now, I am signing off. You are impressive, brave, smart, talented, and everything I have ever wanted, but maybe I met you because you showed me that I can be those things ... that I can be everything I've ever wanted. I don't need to help you chase your dream because I just need to chase mine.

So, fuck you for being the best thing I've ever had, and fuck you for being the worst.

Just like a left-over ice block that's fallen out of
its wrapper from the careless hands of a child onto
hot tarmac in the middle of summer,
you dropped me ...

and I melted.

What happened to my boy,
my sweet boy?
Have you left?
Your shell is here,
but your soul is missing.
It's not you inside.
I don't know this person –
he is confusing,
he's distant.
Standing in front of me with his
authenticity missing,
whispering things
that come from his loins
not his heart.
Was it ever you?
Or were you always a snake
simply buying time
until you shed your skin?

When you're ready, you'll look for me on at the top of mountains, at the bottom of waterfalls, on the back of a boat, inside speeding taxis, wandering big cities, and laid out on a Hawaiian beach. When you're ready ... when reality hits you harder than the alcohol and you realise that my love was genuine ... it was real ... and you were so scared of real that you walked away, only then will you open your eyes, and I won't be beside you. When you're ready, you'll look for me, but it is only when I am ready too ...

that I will find you.

I love you to death, but I need someone worth living for.

I know that when I'm lying awake at 3 a.m., running over our last conversation and trying to pinpoint your last words to me, you are halfway across the world. It's 3 p.m., and you're in a coffee shop, shaking your head because you said my order instead of yours. I know when it's 3 p.m. and I'm at work missing your mid-day calls to ask how my day is going, it's 3 a.m. on the other side of the world, and you're in a bar, talking to a girl and calling her my name by accident. I know that what I felt, you felt. And I know that when I miss you, you miss me even more.

Please drop the front.

BULLY

You built me up,
brick-by-brick
until I stood towering
over the neighbouring buildings.
Undeniably unshaken,
but bricks need concrete
to stick together and
you missed a step.
As soon as
you moved away and
pulled your ladder to the side,

I dismantled like
candy floss.

Today, I found the top I was wearing when I met you. I was sorting out things to donate or throw away. I haven't even seen it since that night. I looked at it, and it looked at me. It had shrunk. It was crinkled, well-worn – even though I'd only worn it once. A bit like you and me, it was almost in good condition but not quite. I instantly thought "throw it out" and went to put it in a big black rubbish bag. Then I thought, "No, it's a nice top. Someone else will use it." I thought of the next girl to put it on … maybe she would wear it with shorts, down a cheap drink, and feel faint from the boy with the crocodile smile instead of the alcohol. I smiled and wished her luck, tossing it in the "give away" pile … a pile I should have tossed us onto. I attempted to move on to the next item, but I stopped and grabbed it back. I held it. I put it back in my wardrobe because I remembered the girl doing her make-up, wondering what to wear, and finding that top. She was anxious and self-conscious and nervous, and if it wasn't for you, I'd still be that girl. But I'm not. And I owe you a lot for that. I never want to throw this experience away. No matter how painful it was – or still is – I never want to forget it. You pushed me to be brave and to be me. Without you, I wouldn't be the girl I am today. And for that, it will never hurt me to see the top I was wearing when I met you.

I will always half-love it, just like I will always half-love you.

Dear Dream Boy,

I don't know if I will ever be able to go to sleep without thinking about you. I don't know if I will ever stop opening my eyes in the dark still trying to see you. You see my boy - you are different. You're ten places at once. You're not just my boy – you're her boy too. You're a southerly wind that sweeps down the road toward me. Even though I cannot see you, I can still feel you kissing the back of my legs. You're invisible. Each night I study your absence, write it out and mind-map it. I connect the dots, draw lines, and analyse where it went wrong and what exit route you took. I spend the night imagining you into existence so that I have some part of you to hold.

When I am tossing and turning in my bed, the planets start talking to me from their resting place. Their words fall like comets. They whisper in my ear and tell me that I am confusing a nightmare for a daydream... they ask me to take a sleeping pill. I am grateful for their concern, but I'm also pissed off. I'm pissed off because even if you're painful, you're *my* painful, but now you're her painful.

Now your hands open a new bedtime story.

Are her pages smoother? Is her plotline funnier? Are the illustrations more interesting? Can she swirl you into a soft slumber better than my story could?

You have a new goodnight kiss and I think that's the part that hurts the most. That each night I crawl into bed without my kiss… I think that is what keeps me up.

You see, I can't fall asleep without you here because if I do, then my day will be ending without you. And without you at the end of my day, I no longer look forward to the next beginning. The next morning, I have to endure knowing you won't be opposite me, drinking your coffee and checking your phone.

It was real, wasn't it? I didn't make this up – you were not a dream … you really were mine. I know you were real because I can still feel you whispering in my ear … placing butterfly kisses on my cheek … wrapping your arms underneath my head. Do you know what happens when I think about you before I fall asleep? I dream about you in a new world – a world where you chose me first … where you called instead of texted … where you didn't walk away when it got hard, and you fought for me. That's the worst bit, I think – that you'll always be my dream boy, but no matter how hard I tried, I was never your dream girl.

So, my dearest dream boy, it is time for me to wake up.

BULLY

You never said it to me, but you never had to – your body language told me. It was in the wind. I felt it, you felt it, and a jet plane shaking in turbulence thousands of miles away did too. I don't need you to say it. I can't say it either, but I can write it.

And so with this, I open the cage I've kept you in, throw the key in the ocean, and stare directly at the sun. Winter warms up, and I start my car. With this, I let you go, and I let myself live. But I'm saying this for us because we never could, I need this somewhere in writing – proof you were real and not just a mirage. I'm letting you go, but I need one last thing to hold onto ...

Always know that no matter what,
I will never stop loving you.

Part Three

DEAR HEART BREAK GIRL,

please use these words as your super glue …

I hate to be the bearer of bad news, but we have a problem here. Maybe you're wrong – maybe he didn't break your heart. Wow! Calm down. I get it. What I'm proposing means all those nights out with your friends, wearing short dresses to prove him wrong ... all those over-analysed messages ... the awkward eye contact ... and the nights in tears were your own fault. Now don't get me wrong – it was awful what he did. It was painful seeing him holding her hand, and even worse, it was excruciating to imagine them side-by-side in bed, skin-to-skin.

I get it. Don't stop listening to me yet. You see, I'm not condoning that kind of behaviour, and I'm very sure the aches in your heart from his careless caresses of other girls are all exceptionally valid. However, what I'm talking about here is how you talk about him. You see, you talk about him like you're talking about a man who puts the stars in the sky ... a man who personally pulls the sun up each morning and who the universe believes is lucky to have on earth. Like yeah, he's okay, but he's not a man – he's a boy. He's another lost boy who's primarily concerned about himself because he's just trying to grow up and find his own way, just like you.

Hey, if you're into someone who gives you their 50% attention and the other 50% to beers with the boys, then I can find a couple hundred more for you to fall in love with. But why are you so especially devastated over this one? It took me a long time to realise that people do not wake up and think, "How am I going to hurt her today?"

Sometimes, things just happen. Sometimes, amongst confusion and life, shit just blatantly hits the fan. Sometimes, people have to lose you to realise they love you, and sometimes, they need to experience other souls in order to entirely want yours.

I grew to learn that when the shit hit the fan ... when he lost interest ... none of it was designed by him to hurt me. He didn't mean it. He just fucked up. So why was I so devastatingly heartbroken? Why do I sit and pour my heart out, longing for a time when the cracks weren't so obvious and I hadn't run out of super glue? Now, here's my idea with this – we custom-make an opposing reality – a situation that runs parallel from our real world. We imagine ourselves with that person, building a future and just doing life together. We want someone to fill our empty spots, and thus we curate this poor human into an avatar of perfection. We make them into someone they're not, simply from the comfort of our own mind. Suddenly, the 17-year-old dropout who's using your English notes and hasn't been accepted into university becomes the love of your life and the smartest man on earth, right? Wrong. Unfortunately for his I-need-petrol-money-can-you-transfer-to-me ass, you've just painted over his true colours with your own colour scheme – different shades of here's-what-I'm-missing-in-my-life-that-I've-decided-you-must-now-represent, and that's that. You're in love. It's not necessarily a bad thing, but it's important to know that you've created not only something that never was, but something that never will be. I have often said to my friends, "You just like the idea of him," and that's the honest truth. It's less about who's in your bed and more about the fact that whoever it is, he is holding your broken pieces together at 2 a.m. – a great service, but a service not always done by the right person for you.

Long story short, be conscious of whether you are crying yourself to sleep over the love of your life or whether you are crying your eyes out over a hyped-up, over-exaggerated version of someone you like. So, maybe he didn't do anything wrong? Maybe you put too much pressure on something that didn't exist in the first place, and what happens when things are under pressure?

They break.

Maybe you made it hard. Maybe you built a castle out of cardboard.

Maybe … you broke your own heart.

Do not mistake the heartbroken for the weak. The heartbroken are the fearless and the unafraid. They laugh at cut glass and dance under lightning strikes for the heartbroken have examined every inch of themselves against their own will. They know what bruises them, and they know what spots to hit to inflict the most pain because they've been hit there themselves. They know how to hide both themselves and the broken pieces. Do not underestimate them because the heartbroken will one day become the heartbreakers.

He ripped down your trust like he was pulling a poster off a wall. So if you are considering giving him a second chance, good luck asking the hands of destruction to rebuild what they already broke.

A gun loaded with a second chance.

His fingers twist around your forearm as he launches to stop you getting in the car. He jerks you back from the door that you had bolted to open, but before he can pull you into him, you spin around and hiss straight in his face, *"Don't you dare touch me! You are never touching me again."* In the heat of the moment, you fling the gun up that you had gripped in your right hand, but now you hold it with two sweaty hands, pointing it straight at his chest. He doesn't jump. In fact, he doesn't even blink. *Does he want this?* In his calmness, you can't help but focus on the sun setting behind him. You think about how similar he is to the sun … rising and setting … leaving you, and then coming back.

Your gut tells you that he isn't scared, and that's the worst part. How can he scare you so much? *"You lying piece of shit,"* you scream, making a move forward as you feel your finger slide around the cold metal trigger. This acts as a litmus test for whether or not he even gives a flying shit. *"Do it,"* he says. *"Fucking do it! Shoot me because I don't want to take one more breath. I don't want to live one more second if it's not with you!"*

What if he planned this whole fucking thing? W*hat if he likes this?* God! Don't you fucking hate how he can predict everything you do? Yeah, maybe you're batshit crazy, but maybe he's the monster who's making you like this. Isn't it cruel how your hands shake but his words don't? You turn the gun around and hold it to your *own chest.*

Oh, so now his face drops ... his tears stop. *Now* he's scared. You see, he's not stupid. He's fully aware that he's a magician with words and able to pull anything out of a hat at the touch of his wand. However, he never thought those kaleidoscope promises would fail him. That's the weird twist, isn't it? And that's what makes him confusing ... the fact that he can manipulate all logic out of you, but simultaneously can't lose you. *"I wish I could live without you,"* you think as you take a deep breath. You pull the trigger.

You knowingly launch a bullet straight into your own heart. It's a shot so deep that the bullet disperses, leaking undeserved hope and forgiveness through your veins. It pulses. You knew the consequences of your actions would be painful, but you didn't care. You endured it anyway – for him. Just like you will endure what he's about to put you through again ... and again ... and again. Because he's worth the pain, isn't he? He's worth putting yourself on the line for, isn't he? You and I both know this isn't his first "second chance". I know you think that you carry this burden for the both of you ... for the good of the relationship. But what is he doing for you?
Nothing.

I pray that one day you'll stop hurting yourself for someone else. Stop giving him another chance at the sacrifice of your own peace. I pray that one day you'll hold that gun up, but instead of being hit with the burden of another second chance, you draw a blank. I pray that one day you'll run out of bullets.

They looked good together. I just don't know why I had to have a front row seat to watch it.

It's like finding out that you have allergies. The report comes back, the doctor shakes his head, and your mum puts her hand on the middle of your back. Devastating news – you're allergic to strawberries … your absolute favourite fruit of all … red, juicy, and sweet. But that horrid rash that spreads across your chest to the tips of your fingers just isn't worth the taste nor the result of you being awake all night, scratching. But when summer crept up and picnic season approached, your hands couldn't help but reach out to grab you a beautiful berry and crunch into it anyway. Now you're older. The report came back, the doctor shook his head, and your mum held your hand. You're allergic to him. Constantly itching and scratching whenever he is near. Your body can't process him. It's a science thing – the genetics are all off here. He's trouble with a capital T, but you bite into him, despite the fact that your organs reject him … your face is swelling … you're unable to swallow … your eyes are puffy and streaming.

It doesn't matter because he's still your favourite.

BULLY

He is not a sculpture.
He is not permanent.
He was not made to be marvelled at.
Nor to have his photo taken.
Don't try to stand him behind ropes.
He is free to go.
You cannot cage him.

Whilst growing up, there will be a handful of times when you truly believe you're in love. The fantastic news is that you are wrong – you are not in love because love doesn't hurt, and you, my child, are hurting. You're playing baseball and trying to get to the next base before getting out. You are running as fast as you can to make it before the ball gets to home. There will be a handful of times growing up when you won't make it in time. You'll lose, skidding your entire body down the ground to hit the square only to watch the ball be caught above you. There is a chance that you've lost recently … or in the past … or you're about to miss the ball in the near future. You're confused because you're confusing a game for emotions. Don't blame this on love because love doesn't lose – love always wins always … and your win is coming soon.

You've been ignoring the facts, and that's okay because facts are scary. But you can't keep living this life of fiction. So, I'm going to tell you this once, and you're going to listen –

He's gone.

And he's not coming back.

Opposites attract. Your genuine heart will meet its counterfeit. Your authenticity will tango with greed, and you, my princess, will kiss your fair share of frogs – frogs that drive fast cars and have comfy hoodies … frogs that don't know what they want but know they enjoy your light and decide they need to keep sucking on it. Maybe for a couple of weeks, these frogs will pull disappearing acts only to remember how good you are at that thing they like. They will come back. Stop putting these frogs (boys … people before yourself because it's a waste of energy. By placing your energy into the wrong things, you are watering the wrong garden. You are sitting on the wrong Lilly pad - in the wrong pond.

You are waiting for a change, but you will be waiting forever because he's not the one. He's not capable of being what you want. He can't give you what you deserve, and he can't handle your passion. Transformation can't happen without magic which is why he keeps coming back to you. You have something he is desperate for – power. The power to create change. You're witchcraft, love potion, swirling wands, and expensive ingredients. You can make him better than he currently is - and he knows that. Don't give it to him. He is undeserving. Stop trying to transform someone who is incapable of becoming what you need. The books are wrong – frogs do not transform into princes, they turn into toads.

Stop kissing boys and expecting them to grow up.

Love is not immortal.

And that is a brutal lesson to learn at such a young age.

The cute ones always know what to say.

Instead, go for a quiet one who looks in your eyes and makes you forget words even exist.

If he was meant to be yours, this wouldn't be happening. You wouldn't fall asleep cuddling doubt. You wouldn't have to check his Facebook and his Instagram … you wouldn't feel constantly insecure … you wouldn't have to ask his friends if they are with him… or who he's with…he wouldn't have claw marks on his back from your nails trying to hold onto him.

And if he was meant to be yours, you wouldn't be reading this book.

I found a tiger walking the earth in a human body. Despite his broad shoulders marked with alternating stripes, he did not scare me. I thought he was cute – a pussy cat. I liked cats. Shaking his hand, he accepted my invitation to come back to my place later for a drink. We sat on my couch before starting a tour of my bedroom. His tongue was rough. He licked me all over, installing my feet into a frensy of kicking. It tickled so terribly, and I couldn't stop laughing. He got carried away and nipped me gently, but he was quick to kiss the spot. The only light in the room glowed from his golden eyes – my night light. His fur was soft like a baby blanket which distracted me from how sharp his teeth were. He was elegant and different, and he was hungry. You will possibly not be surprised to learn that his teeth burned whiter, hotter, and closer … until they sank into my jugular, ripping me from the spot in my neck he previously sucked in love.

I convinced myself it was safe. I told myself he was harmless, but he was, is, and always will be a tiger … a hunter … a killer. He eats meat, and I put myself on a silver platter. I saw a predator and offered myself up as prey. I stumbled upon a roaming tiger, and he dragged me into his corner of the world. But I knew it was going to happen – I looked danger in the eye and gave it a glass of wine.

Do not make excuses for his behaviour.

Isn't it funny how he only wants you back when your back is arched against someone new?

You can still feel it, can't you? His hand holding yours while he pressed down on the clutch, accelerating down the highway. You can still remember it, can't you? When he picked you up in his car for the first time. You can still feel your red blood cells rising to the top of your skin to meet his fingertips. You can still feel his hands sliding down, pulling back your jeans and the layers you had grown to keep out the world. These memories give you food poisoning – nausea from the outside in. No matter how hard you try, his initials still spiral to the front of your brain just like you used to write in the night air with sparklers as a child.

If you're wondering why you can't stop thinking about him - there is your answer. You're thinking about him because you don't want him to stop thinking about you. And he never will. He will remember you just like you remember him – passionately. You'll remember each other because you two proved that love was real, that the romantic comedies weren't trash, the novels weren't exaggerated, and your parent's marriage wasn't an accident. You guys really did it. You found softness in a hard world. You baked a cake without a recipe and with no idea of what it was going to turn out like, you mixed in half a cup of time, a quarter cup of focus, a teaspoon of jealousy, and a litre of trust, and you made it.

You made love.

That deserves to be remembered.

I was afraid of clowns throughout my entire childhood, and then I grew up and dated them instead.

You talk about him like he puts the stars in the sky, but they shine even brighter without him here.

I think that's pretty ironic, don't you?

Every time he kisses her, shakes someone's hand, introduces himself, buys a drink, checks another girl out, gets home drunk, sits down at the movies, or stands in the middle of a crowded room,

he is looking for you.

Perhaps you love incomplete people because you have never completely loved yourself.

It doesn't matter — how it ended, what he said, who he's with, where he lives now, if you saw his mum in the supermarket, what his best friend said to your friend to tell you, if he blocked you, if he didn't, if he texted you on your birthday, or if he liked your photo. It doesn't matter. What matters is the fact that you're waiting for a car to pull into your driveway, and that car isn't coming. What's going to happen is that you're going to look out the window of your bedroom every day at 8:45 p.m., waiting for him to get back from practice and he's not going to be there. You're going to wear his t-shirt to bed. You're going to wake up the next morning and reach out for him, and he won't be there. You're going to drive to university and take the turnoff to his house by accident. What is going to happen is that you're going to miss him. But none of this matters because he is going to be replaced. By someone who doesn't ditch you for the boys… someone who stays the night and someone who has got better intentions. Now that doesn't mean that your first love wasn't great because being scared is great. Being young and kissing someone in the rain at your favourite concert wearing his hoodie is great, but the real thing won't be that messy. Real love won't make you lose your appetite. Real love won't run away from you, and it will naturally fall into your lap. Real love is a giver - it will give you what you give to it. Release your grip on the first. You don't need to hold onto him and what went wrong. None of it matters because he was not yours to have, he was yours to borrow, but you deserve someone to keep… and he's on his way.

I grew up doing anything I could to make the boys I loved happy. I watched every one of them do whatever they needed and wanted to make themselves happier than I ever could. How naive I was to give my happiness to someone else who didn't even want it.

Why not keep it for myself?

You applied clay masks, picked at your blackheads, popped your pimples, and exfoliated the oils on top of your cheeks. You treated him as if he was sebum oozing from your skin. You tried to rid yourself, shed yourself, reveal yourself, but you cannot extract him because despite what it feels like...

he is no longer inside you.

He never will be again.

Fuck it. Fuck his chain and his cool new jeans. Fuck that his playlists are better than yours. Fuck that he can skateboard. Fuck that it's fun having sex in the back of his car. Fuck what he said he'd do but didn't. Fuck his birthday party that everyone's going to. Fuck his jawline when he clenches it. Fuck the fact that he's on the top sports team. Fuck the fact he's a year older than you. Fuck that you like his friends. Sometimes, you truly just have to say, "Fuck it!" Say, "Fuck it," and go fuck someone better.

That's what I learnt about moving on ... it's instantaneous. I thought it was the most complex topic of all – an antidote requiring over 100 ingredients (all organic).

Moving on is not strict - it's simple.

Moving on is a yes or no. It's going to a party without wanting to bump into him. It's looking at other guys and not wanting to see him. It's meeting new people instead of always trying to find someone as close to the one you just lost.

Moving on is like skipping rope, sometimes you trip, sometimes you get it perfect, but the whole time you are exhausted, and you know that it is going to end.

It is a choice to keep suffering.

So choose! Stop trying to jump rope, there is no point, no goal, and it will go on forever until you decide to simply not jump any longer until you decide.

Decide to walk away finally.

Decide it isn't worth it.

You tell yourself that you can change him, but why should he have to change at all?

If it was right, it wouldn't need to be any different.

You have put a lot of pressure on boys – to be your home … to be your comfort … to be your value system … to make you feel worthy.

Boys are just boys.

No one likes to feel pressure, not even you. It is not his job to make you feel better about yourself just because you think he's cute.

To every girl crying in a taxi on the way home and wearing the jewellery he gave you when you go to sleep, know that this pain is temporary.

To every lost girl, I promise you – you're going to be found.

He chose her.
Now you need to choose yourself.

On the day he left, he woke up before I did and much earlier than usual. He must have set a silent alarm. He tiptoed out of bed to brush his teeth, then shortly after, he picked up a long-woven rope in his left hand whilst sliding open the back door with his right. Dewdrops fell alongside the morning light as he twisted the rope above him. He flung it with all his might high into the sky, far past the clouds in order to haul her from her home. He heaved the sun down from her ascent to the top of the earth. He snatched her up, putting her screaming, kicking, and crying into a bag. He stole the day.

My alarm didn't go off at the normal time. Two hours later, I drowsily awoke to no daylight, just more darkness. Pulling my curtains back, I only discovered the same – never-ending nothingness. I sat down alone in the middle of oblivion with no company other than the tearful moon and confused clouds. We didn't know what to do. He had left and taken life as I knew it with him … my schedule, routine, beliefs, joys, but worst of all – my happiness.

He bundled them all up and escaped. But he forgot one thing – the sun. She shines, and like a trail of breadcrumbs, a line-up of sunbeams had formed a pathway behind him. I could find him. It wasn't so much that I wanted him back, but I wanted her. And with that, I ran as fast as my legs could carry me until my feet where planted in front of his letter box and my thighs where quivering. No second attempt was needed.

All it took was one blow to smack down his front door. I towered above him, holding his head firmly between my hands.

"I have come for the sun."

He cried out from between my grip, begging for forgiveness … telling me that she'd already left … that he wasn't strong enough to hold her … that she had already come in search of me. Between the dark curtains gleamed a small ray – one simple bolt of light that crept through like a kid sneaking into the living room on Christmas morning. Simply and within seconds, the ray grew brighter, and soon, the whole world lit up.

I was naive to doubt her. Of course, he couldn't contain her. How could I believe that a simple boy was strong enough to steal the sun? How could I believe that a simple boy was strong enough to steal my happiness?

Dedicated to Rupi Kaur,
who has unknowingly taught me to follow
my dreams for the last two years.

You have a smile that feels like home. That is why he tries to rebuild the house even after he has demolished it, and that's why you need to be more careful about who you keep as a tenant.

Not everyone deserves keys to your front door.

Your trust issues are as deep as the apology you never got.

This might be unbelievable to you, but he didn't mean to do it. He really did love you, but he had a short attention span, and she was glossy. Soon, she will also seem dull to him. His eyes will dart to find the next glimmer. He is a magpie – always chasing objects, never considering its substance. He is a man who wants an accessory - not a woman. Despite this, I know he was wonderful, and he made you feel wonderful. You guys had it all worked out, like the first house you were going to buy - the one with the driveway and the white fence. It was close to work with the spare room to be painted pink or blue one day. He took you to his cousin's wedding ... he showed you off ... he was interested in things you were interested in ... he was your safety... he was the answer to your problems ... he showed you new songs and took photos of you when you weren't watching ... he was everything you'd ever wanted. And then, he changed his mind. He wanted a new toy. He fucked up. He slid a knife across your back. He prioritised everything else above you. You thought he was the one, and he was – he was the one to highlight your strengths by showing you your weaknesses and the one to teach you what being wanted feels like because he wanted other girls more than he wanted you. He was the one to show you that you deserve a lot better. You are not an accessory to be added to an outfit when it looks good. You are not a sometimes girl. You are a chandelier dripping diamonds and light. You deserve a permanent place in someone's heart.

Your future is not worried about whether he's in it or not.

Know that he was young and didn't think things through. There's a part of him that looks at girls like a 4-year-old looks at butterflies. He wants to catch them, hold them, and play with them, but then he'll get bored and throw them away. He gave you up for a girl whose name he forgot after she said it ... a 5-minute girl ... a girl who tastes like plastic.

But I can promise you this, he will regret it. Plastic gets old quickly. Plastic melts. Authenticity doesn't. You are real and you were it, one in a million, a forever girl – the kind of girl you want to wake up to every morning for the rest of your life ... the kind you want to take home on Christmas Day... the kind of girl you buy art for... the kind of girl you take to the other side of the world, and the kind of girl that changes lives.

You don't know what you've got till it's gone, so go and leave him and his stubbornness to figure out that he just made the biggest mistake of his life.

If you keep looking for someone to lean on, you will always be out of balance.

There is nothing wrong with you. He didn't choose her because you lacked a quality. He has grown up using his fingers as cages, and that is why he picked her because you were too much of a good thing and his hands couldn't trap your soul. He is with her because he can dominate her mind more than he can dominate yours. You don't need to be with someone for the sake of being with someone, but she does. She is with him out of fear, the fear of losing him and losing comfort.

You are not afraid of people leaving you, and you don't need anyone to keep you on track. Your life is meaningful without help which is why he's with her.

He couldn't handle that you didn't need him to make you whole.

Continuously trying to make someone fit when they aren't supposed to only means never finishing the jigsaw.

Sometimes the universe doesn't fight for people to be together. Sometimes you've got to fight for each other, and for that to happen, you need someone who recognises that you're worth fighting for.

You are wasting your time posting pictures and hoping he'll like them … talking to his friends and hoping they will tell him.… going out drinking just to prove you're having fun … talking about how successful your new job is in the hopes he'll hear... going on dates with boys at the cafe he sometimes visits.

You're trying to impress someone who couldn't even show up to dinner on time. You're wasting your time trying to make someone who wasted his chance with you jealous.

Re-evaluate.

He reached for you when the clouds grew heavy, formatting themselves into an unbreakable order. Their tears fell like raindrops, flooding the footpath. He glanced out the window and saw his saturated surroundings. He laced his boots and pulled you out of the stand to resurrect you up above him. You were his protection when danger was near – his shield … his armour. You were his umbrella, and he didn't think twice before sacrificing you to the cold in order to keep himself dry.

Let him miss you as much as you missed him.

If he was your soulmate, he wouldn't be destroying your soul and hitting on your mate.

Remember when you were five and you tripped in a water park, landing on unforgiving concrete and scraping your knee so badly it felt like the most agonizing stabbing pain that would never ever end? Remember how your mum put a dinosaur plaster on it every day, and you would touch the top of it at school to test how badly it ached as compared to the day before? You don't remember taking the final plaster off, but you remember looking down a few weeks later at your knee and seeing the fresh new skin there as if nothing had ever happened. Now you're 18, and your heart's been broken. You're mum can't understand why you don't get out of bed some mornings and other nights you don't ever go to sleep. You plaster over the pieces with the alcohol that your older friend brought you and the lips of a boy you don't even want. Each day you look at a picture of him or reread old texts just to touch the scrape and test how much it aches compared to the day before. With every day that goes by, it will hurt and hurt and hurt, and then suddenly, you're dancing at a bar with your best friends or under the stars at 3 a.m. or merely walking down the footpath with your headphones on, and suddenly, it doesn't hurt anymore. You never remember taking the final plaster off, but eventually, it is as if nothing ever happened. You'll think about how quickly things heal, and even though at the time you got the scrape you thought you'd never feel better, randomly, and suddenly … you do. It is not the time that heals the wound. It is you – your own skin and blood – that mends the cut. It is no different whether you are eight or eighteen.

You will fix yourself.

Be careful.

Attention and love are two different things. You mistake them for one another and that's why you're over thinking.

You're attached to the amount of time someone is giving to you, when it's the quality of time that matters the most.

Keep going, not for you but for your future self. There is a future you who is so in love she wakes up smiling. There is a future you, sitting on top of the kitchen table, wearing an oversized t-shirt that smells like cologne and laughter, listening to good music with a spoon in her hand sharing chocolate cake with the love of her life. That future you, well … she can't even remember the boy who is twisting your universe like liquorice right now.

Keep going.

Keep getting through this heartbreak … for her.

Dear Heartbreak Girl,

Look, you need stability in a relationship – not one that flip-flops around where it's "I love you!" today and "I hate you!" tomorrow. To be totally honest, you are in this kind of relationship now. You are in "victim and villain roles." Realise you're in it together. Accept neither of you are the enemy. Don't allow him to take advantage of you. Once a person notices you are no longer within reach, they tend to realise your unavailability and reconsider wanting you in their life. When the ball is in your court, assume home court advantage. Don't cause a turnover and give your opponent the ball too easily – make him work for it. I know you will think of him when you're in bed watching a movie or Wednesday or in the fucking shower, but right now, you need to put your game face on. We all have weak moments, but you are a strong person. Even if you feel like you are in a bad place, stand up for yourself. Push through it. No matter how scared you are, you cannot let him have the power to make you sad or lonely. Remember that broken cannot fix broken. You need to learn to be super happy in your own life. Focus every cell in you on this and fix yourself first before you attempt to fix him. Some of the things that hurt us actually heal us. Some of the things that confuse us actually give us the answer. Sometimes rejection is redirection to something better. You are where you are for a reason. Time to focus on you, girl! You are worth a lot more than how he is treating you. Always here …

Love, Cass xx

Part Four

THE SECOND LOVE

Hand him a screw driver.
He is here to dismantle the first.

BULLY

I presented to you my first love.
You put it in a gift box.
You tied it up in string,
covered it in wrapping paper,
stuck a name tag
on the top.
Finished it off with a ribbon,
in one final knot,
it was done.

You made it look so beautiful.
How easy it was for me to
move on
after you tied up,

all the Loose Ends.

I knew I'd met you before. Your hands felt familiar. Your eyes too warm to be a stranger, but it was that smile more than anything. Oh, yes – I could see that smile from a mile away. I wasn't wrong. You can't blame me. Because you and I, kid, we've walked through many lifetimes together. You see, there's been a you and a me in every phase of evolution … swinging in the roaring 20s … drinking whiskey and watching the stock market crash during the 30s … waving goodbye through train windows in the 40s … writing love letters to and from wars in the 50s … and marching for peace, wearing bold flares with flowers in our hair in the 60s. Every decade has known a me and a you, side-by-side, fighting for what was right and what we loved.

I don't know what went so wrong this time. I don't know why we fought against love instead of for it. This round just isn't for us, baby. Our road maps aren't intersecting anymore, but instead, they are leading us in opposite directions. We are magnets, and I knew I'd find you. But this time, we are repelling away from each other instead of attracting toward each other. It hurts. I'm sad too. But I'll tell you this, there's a you and there's a me … sitting under a tree on a wharf in Greece … on a boat in the Mediterranean … laid out on a grass hill under the stars … in a buggy in the middle of a desert. A you and a me, holding each other's hand in a simple church … standing at the altar with blue flowers lining the aisle. Oh, yes – I can see it now. I can see a me, and I can see a you. And all I know is, I'm saying I do.

Church bells rang as I screamed your name on a mid-Sunday morning.

Your tongue is holy.

BULLY

You pushed into me and
simultaneously,
far away
in the furthest layer of the atmosphere,
two meteors collided.

They fractured each other.
A pleasurable pain.

For when we made love
the universe did too.

I can pretend to pray for peace, love, health, and harmony, but I know as well as you do that all I have ever wanted is him. If my world fell apart and I was merely holding his hand, that would be all the reassurance I needed.

Your eyes are my waterfall – when they blink, I drown.

Out of everything that new love brings, nothing will ever make me happier than what new feelings do to transform the night time. When you are loveless and in your regular routine, the night is merely a time machine to the next day – the start of the next scheduled section of tasks, chores, and changes. And then one day, you meet someone … you stumble onto them … walk into them … or maybe you open your eyes, and they have been sitting in front of you this whole time. With that meeting, the night time opens up like a theme park that's been shut down ever since the last time you felt like this. The wheels turn, the lights spark, and well-dressed clowns on stilts emerge. Animals crawl out of the bushes, and the candy floss machine starts twirling.

Each night, you line up and purchase a different type of ticket. Sometimes your night brings passion, other times understanding, good conversations, funny conversations, deep conversations, spontaneous decisions, adventures you didn't expect, or silences that mean more than words. Lions roar from cages … you get forced onto roller coasters you don't want to go on … you eat too much sugar … your feet get tired, but the adrenaline keeps you going. You know it's going to end the whole time, but it seems to last the perfect span of forever … forever until it's over in a split second. Then suddenly, you can't experience the day the same. You can't talk the same or see things the same, and you have to pretend like your life wasn't changed the night before. You have to walk through the day and act normal, but then your phone lights up, you get that text from him, and you can hear the carnival music in the back of your head.

That's what I love about new love. It rewires you, it revitalises you, and it gives you a new dose of fun. Your sleep schedule is fucked up, your heart is fucked up, and the things you're whispering at 3 a.m. are probably fucked up too. Enjoy it all – enjoy the danger and the unknown. But do me a favour – double-knot your shoelaces before you run ahead … double-check the safety harnesses on the rides … do your seatbelt up extra tight on the bumper cars. Indulge, but don't overdo it. And it's okay if you get lost in his eyes, but don't forget your mum's picking you up later.

Not all theme parks are genuine. They are overly saturated, masked, a mirage, and it's important that you don't wear your heart on your sleeve. Keep some cards close to your chest, and if he leaves you half-way through the night like the last one did, then know it's okay to shut the rollercoaster down and lay there alone, blinking at the stars and wondering how on earth you've gone from missing someone at 3 a.m. to losing someone at 3 a.m. to forgetting that 3 a.m. exists, and finally, to waiting for someone to come home. Lions and tigers and bears, candy and cotton and fears, out of everything that brand-new love brings, nothing will make me happier than the terror of not knowing what's going to transform next.

Take the air from my lungs, but just leave me with his hands.

My heart needed a renovation.
The ceilings were cracked,
and the exterior well-worn.
An update was overdue.

Thank you for being my architect.

"I feel like this whole night I was watching a movie, and I kept trying to pause it."

"Why pause it?"

"To make it last longer." My fingers tried to pull away, but he grabbed my hand back firmly into his, "Do you know what you remind me of?"

"What?"

"That time I went sky diving... I was so nervous. I didn't know what was going to happen. I waited and waited, I was taken up in a plane and I looked out over the rolling world. I remember thinking I'd never seen anything so beautiful and simultaneously never been so scared. All I wanted to do was be consumed by it, but I didn't know if it was safe. The anticipation built up until it was unbearable. I questioned myself... Could I do it? Could I survive? Maybe my parachute won't open. It might be the best experience of my life or the worst. I might get hurt. Was I ready?"

"Why does that remind you of me?"

"Because I was scared of what it might turn into, I was excited, I didn't know what would happen – if I would fall or fly but regardless

– I jumped."

We could run away somewhere – alone. I could make you forget about everything, and you could be my home.

I was in battle with my body but to you,

I surrendered it.

Love to me was like donating blood.
You were generous if you gave it,
everyone needed it,
some people didn't have enough,
they required help.

Giving was kind
- taking was scary.
You didn't want to lose it.

I thought people had a
love quota
like they could only bleed so much
before they ran out.

Then I met you,
you pulled the drip out of my arm,
you told me softly that...

*"Love is Endless,
there is no running out of it."*

That I didn't need yours
or anyone else's
to survive.

For I already had it
running through my system,
all along.

"You write poetry."

I was standing in front of him, putting make-up on in the mirror. I snapped from my lip liner to his eyes. He was sitting behind me, leaning forward, not blinking, fingers laced, his elbows on his knees and a half-smile on his face – very confident in the approach.

"And how do you know that ?"

The half-smile grew to a full smile. My half-butterflies merged into a swarm of wasps which plummeted to the depths of my organs.

"I don't know it. I can hear it – you remember the details ... like what candy I like or the colour of my toothbrush. I can see it – because you show it on your face and in your eyes. See your words do not only come from your hands... oh no, you write words with your very presence. You write with your lips. I can feel the letters when I kiss you. You've always got something to say, but it is not your voice that wants to tell me – it is your body. That is why you like my hands so much because I can't hear you unless I undress you."

"No, I like your hands because my body to you is like touch typing. You have the placement memorised. Your eyes are unnecessary to your success - you don't even need to look to know what keys to hit...

your hands make my body talk. "

He chuckled, stood up, and started walking towards me. Panic.

"That's what I mean – you never directly told me you write poetry. But listen to what you just said ... that's the most beautiful and vulnerable shit I've ever heard. How could I not pick up on that? Listen to the words that come out of your mouth."

"You think you know everything. You think you've got me exactly where you want me, but you can't read me as well as you think you can. I'm not that predictable."

"Oh, fuck – of course you're not. You're a writer."

"Exactly, so don't assume anything."

"Why?"

"Because I'll just change the ending."

He grabbed my hips and pulled me up onto my toes.

"And what makes you think this is ever going to end?"

I would give you the sky, but I can't reach that high. I would give you the ocean, but my arms can't stretch that wide. I would give you the mountains, but I'm not that strong. Instead, I'll give you me – my heart and a key.

For if I gave you the world, it would go so wrong, but I am yours to keep and I secretly hope that *that* is what you wanted all along.

BULLY

You showed me
that the sun would continue to rise
each morning
even though I no longer woke up beside him.
You were different.
You woke me up by
making love to me
instead of taking it away,
and that was the key difference...

he Took,
and you Gave.

It wasn't what I imagined it would be like. It wasn't like the movies. It wasn't polished. He didn't compliment me endlessly. We didn't talk about our feelings much, but when we did, he looked away and said, "Look, I just really like you."

It wasn't walking on clouds, instead he brought me back down to earth. He asked me about my writing when he could see the bags under my eyes from a late night. He watched my TV show instead of his. He called me on his lunch break, just so I could tell him about my day and moan about my meetings. He always asked my opinion first. He sent me photos of tattoos I'd like. It wasn't pretty words instead it was him laughing as he said, "I hate you." It wasn't easy. It was hard. It took effort. It was scary. It was opening doors I didn't want to open in order to introduce him to the skeletons no one else had met. It was thinking about him walking home from work or driving to each other's house after our parents fell asleep.

It was laughing at mistakes, getting lost, losing contact, and finding our way back. It was nerves. It was sweaty palms.

It was "I miss you" and "I'm sorry".
It was undeniable …

It was love.

BULLY

I traveled the world
only to find that all I wanted to see ...

was you.

If I tell you that I have feelings for you, then I will be saying it out loud, and that makes it real, and I don't want it to be real. I would rather it stay in my head. You see, it is safe there. I'm scared to tell you the truth, in case something goes wrong afterwards but I'm even more afraid that maybe something will go right. Maybe you'll stay. Maybe you'll love me back. Maybe you walk down the street thinking about what happened that night too. Maybe it was as good for you as it was good for me. Maybe your heart beats faster when you hear my name, and perhaps you count the seconds until you see me again, but in case you don't, I'll love you in my head.

You will be my snow globe – suspended in water with small flakes of white frost floating around you when shaken. I will keep you on my windowsill, that way you will always be available when I need to glance at you in small doses. I will keep you there in your best state as a constant reminder that I will always have you with me. The truth is every piece of me is yours, and I can't imagine the future without you. I won't ever forgive myself if I let the glass break.

So just in case, your version of forever is not as long as mine. I will keep a stone figure of your body.

Our love suspended for eternity.

No one has a "type". You do not respond to people just because they are over a certain height or have a certain eye colour or a university degree in a certain subject. The people you love in your life will come in different forms. Stop creating your curated list. You think you know what you want, but you don't.

Meeting him was the moment I was proven wrong. After all of that – that extensive criteria I laid out – I met him, and he made me feel like myself.

And that's it. That's all there is to it.

You're going to have a moment like me one day where suddenly, this one person is going to be everything you ever wanted him to be without even knowing you wanted it at all.

"Don't look back, okay?" I threw my legs over the balcony railing, lowering myself down.

"Obviously." He followed, closing the window behind us.

"Promise?" I asked through heavy breaths and a half-smile.

"Promise." He grabbed my hand and squeezed.

And with that, I launched my back off the bush that was covering us and ran as fast as I could, heels swinging from my right hand and him from my left. We didn't look to see if anyone at the party could see us sprinting across the grass, but their small talk flickered in my ears, motivating me to run as far away from them as possible. I had no fucking desire to remain part of that for any longer than absolutely necessary, and the couple of hours we'd managed to keep our hands off one another was long enough.

We dived into darkness, letting each other go and sprinting down the brick path. My gold dress was in my hands as we went smashing through a handful of rosemary bushes and a wishing well. Hurtling toward the end of the garden, we finally saw our target – the outdoor marquee. We were on track for success … until the automatic lights turned on.

"What was that?? Is someone there?"

I could hear them, and it slowed me down. Escaping a party shoeless and with a boy in hand wasn't exactly an ideal exit. But surprisingly, he did what he'd promised (possibly for the first time in his life), and without a second thought, he pulled me forward, flinging us onto the outdoor couch, rolling on top of each other. His hands quickly wrapped around my waist – safety and success. My body relaxed underneath his, and my hands twisted in his hair. But as any romantic would do, I looked past him. I looked at the sky because the stars were laughing so loudly I couldn't ignore them any longer. Finally, I laughed back at them. I loved to hate them. How dare they have this planned the whole time?!

"And what are you laughing at?" He pulled my thighs into him.

"The stars."

"Hmm, and what did they do?" His lips pressed against my neck. Kissing was a go-to goose-bump mechanism for me and entertainment for him.

I couldn't help but smile through my squinted eyes. I couldn't help but enjoy having the knowledge of something that he didn't. He was distracted, but my brain couldn't stop spinning. His teeth dragged down to my collar bone, taking my dress strap with them.

"I'm scared," I blurted out.

His face snapped up, "Of what?"

Anxiety pulsing through me, I panicked. I don't know why I can't think of how to explain anything in person … like ever … *"How about I write you something?"*

"How do you do that?" He rested his head on my chest. "Like, can you actually just remember everything to write about? Everything in a moment just like this?"

"I already have. I remember every part of moments like this."

He grinned. "You know, I read something that reminded me of you. It said if you've fallen in love with a writer, then you'll live forever."

His lips went back to their pathway down my torso … *"Have you already fallen in love with me then?"* I squeezed his hips between my thighs.

"Hey!" His grip tightened, and my thighs weakened. He pushed himself back up, so we were face-to-face with his eyes staring straight into mine …

"Don't look back, remember?"

I will love you when you are wrong ... when you're using your hands too often when you talk just to make your point. I will love you when you raise your voice at me because you're frustrated. I will love you when you are stressed and take it out on me by accident. I will love you when you snap back at me for no reason. I will love you when you've gained a few pounds after your birthday from eating too much of your favourite desert. I will love you when you get an idea and decide to peruse a new hobby (like the time you got into yoga). I will love you when you're bad at yoga. I will love you when you spend too much at the bar on a night out with the boys. I will love you when you lose your patience. I will love you when you lie to me about going to strip clubs (it was a stag-do – I get it). I will love you when you don't know your next move yet. I will love you when you're on the couch, and I'm paying the bills. I will love you when you go back on your medication. I will love you when you come off it. I will love you when you forget your purpose. I will love you when you feel useless. I will love you when you forget to do the dishes. I will love you when you demand we watch your show instead of mine for the second night in a row. I will love you when you're high. I will love you when you're sober. I will love you when you doubt yourself and everything you create. I will love you when you think you're not good enough. I will love you when you get home late and you're too tired to talk. I will even love you when you're secretive. I will love you when the world brings you down because I know that my love will bring you back up.

Her lips twisted up … smiling, fingers intertwined, eye shadow smudged down her cheek. Her mouth was wet. She was the most fantastically obvious paradox. Desperate, but deserving. Smart, but needy. Beautiful, but deadly. I loved it when she sang against the sheets. I felt like a composer. Her body arched, legs apart and hands gripping the pillow like she was trying to hold onto sanity … or maybe just hold onto this moment. That's all she wanted – a love to hold onto in a world that kept telling her to let it go.

You told me I had clear skin when I wasn't wearing make-up, and you were looking at my acne scars. You told me I looked pretty with my hair unbrushed … flawless wearing just a towel … sexy curled up in a big shirt and socks. You looked at me the same way, regardless of whether it was 8 a.m. before I'd had a shower or it was 8 p.m. and I was dressed up to go to dinner.

That's when I realised, you saw something in me that I couldn't see in myself.

That's when I realised, you saw me for who I have always wanted to be - my best self.

You peeled off a layer of skin to reveal who you were. The person behind all the glitz and the fast cars, behind the lights and mics, and behind the designer sneakers and chains. You gave me what you've never given anybody else – yourself. You took off the mask and held out your pain.

Is that why you keep coming back to me again and again?

Your touch is an eraser, and you're rubbing his fingerprints off me.

New hands.

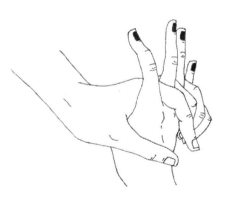

Your teeth bit down gently onto the skin between my breasts, and in the gaps of your teeth, I found the closure I needed to move on from one love to the next.

I would tell you about the planets — how the moons orbits and all about outer space, but words to you were trivial. It was your body that shut my lips up. I talked about the stars but you are the one who actually took me there.

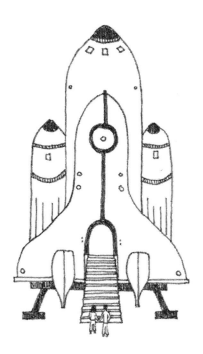

My parents tell stories of their lives before kids, like when they missed their flight home or when my Dad got a stomach bug at a dinner party. I wonder if that will be us one day, sitting around on a Sunday morning, drinking coffee, and telling our babies the stories that we are living right now – like how we accidently wore costumes to a party that wasn't dress up or when we stole your mother's car and drove as far away from the city as we could. If only our stories were like this book – printed, tangible, and able to be flicked over. I wish I could cheat and turn to the last page to see if it is really you in the end.

Your lips look like light, and when they touch me, I start shining.

Addicted.

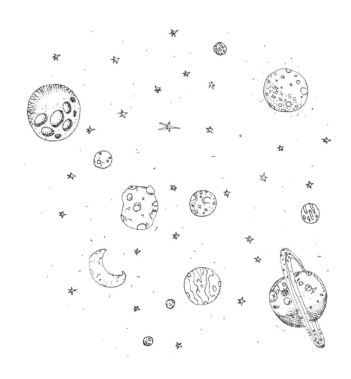

He asked me about you today …

"What does he do that I didn't?"

"Don't even get me started. He takes me seriously. He doesn't hang out with me just to get something in return. He puts me first. He looks at my eyes not my chest. He asks me what I want to do. He remembers the small things. He kisses me when I least expect it. He introduces me to his friends, shows me off, and wants to be seen with me. He plays my music in the car. He makes an effort and takes the time to learn about my mind. He's interested in what I'm doing. He wants me to succeed. He isn't selfish, and he is genuine with his feelings. Look, if you really want to know what he does that you didn't, he makes me a priority."

The answer to that question was far easier than I lead on, it was simple *"everything."*

The ocean which separated us has endlessly watered our love, making it overgrown. I called the gardener to cut the hedges back to make it more manageable. He swung his axe unsuccessfully at your branches that are comfortably twisted around the chambers of my pumping blood, but the roots were too deep and thorns too sharp. I looked under the bark and found the sprouts of my ripe heart, and this is a credit to you. For it is only with your love inside me that I flourished, regardless of where I was buried - no oxygen required. For as long as I have you in my heart, I am constantly evolving.

My darling boy our distance means we have grown reckless with our love, careless with our kisses and although they will try to pick us apart, they will never be able to cut us down.

All this sky that is separating us makes it difficult to love you. However, to me, distance is not a challenge because the further away you are, the harder I fall. Now for you, I will stop falling, and I will learn to fly.

You kissed every insecurity and stuck it back together like super glue.

It is no surprise that I'm so attached to you.

He threw me on top of the speakers whilst whispering in my ear that my body was the greatest song he'd ever heard, and he likes his music loud.

I rolled over, and you were beside me, and that was the first morning I woke up and didn't want to go back to sleep again.

When I was younger, I liked the bad boys … the fast cars with no registrations and the ones that brought you in the back door instead of the front door so they didn't have to introduce you to their mum. I pretended to like bands that I didn't like, and I bum-puffed cigarettes in one-size-too small denim short-shorts to impress them. I liked the bad boys because they would look at the girl next to them for a few seconds longer than they should while still holding my hand. They made me feel reckless, uncertain, and flustered, but they were unpredictable. And to me, that was what entertained me.

I grew older, and I decided I liked the intellectual boys – the ambitious ones … the ones with reading glasses, empty cups of coffee, white sneakers, and absolutely no time to possibly schedule an hour to see me … the ones who forgot everything I said because their top priority was themselves and their second priority was their success. Not a bad thing, but I was not included. I liked that because they made me feel insignificant which made me want to improve – get better, be smarter, and work harder. I thought maybe if I was as dedicated to something like them, then maybe that would persuade them to be committed to me. They were successful, scary, and predictable, but they were safe.

And then I met you, and you showed me that bad boys can have good intentions and soft kisses … that even if they drive fast cars, they always open the door for you. You told me about your mum with the light of love glowing from your heart. You hate smoking. You showed me that a bad boy can also be an intellectual boy who's street smart and not just book smart. I like that. I like pulling your glasses off before I pull your shirt off. You showed me that ambitious people are only as busy as they allow themselves to be, and no matter what, work — although important — doesn't have to be your top priority. You made me your top priority. You showed me that success doesn't mean arrogant or cocky. In fact, success can create humility and courtesy. You made me feel significant regardless of what was going on. You told me I didn't have to have it all sorted out to improve, and I didn't need to be anyone other than myself to hold your focus.

You presented our love like a billboard — wrote your commitment in bold letters, glued it down, and swung it above our city for the entire town to read.

You showed me that it is possible to have a love that is proud.

"You and I,
we are like a highway in the sky.
You can't see the road,
but you know it's going somewhere."

I think about you when it rains because you like stormy weather which is ironic because you are anything but dark and gloomy. Overall, I think that is one of your greatest assets. You somehow always make the worst into the best. You make a tough situation rewarding. You make chaos organised. You make solutions out of problems, and you make everyday things entertaining. And now because of you, I look forward to grey skies and even hurricanes. Because on that day, you proved to me that you are good at driving through storms, and I think that only added to my admiration for you. How can someone so positive enjoy all the negatives? I do not despair now when I see clouds on the weather forecast. I see clouds and think of your hand holding mine to your lips and you kissing each one of my fingers as the heavens open up and the windscreen wipers work on overdrive. You couldn't have been less phased at the change in conditions – which you made sure I knew as your eyes were still glued on mine. And despite the fact you weren't looking at the road, the car was somehow still driving straight in the right direction. You didn't blink – which I understood because I couldn't look away either. Now, every time I hear rain on my window or on my umbrella or roof, I think about how maybe – just maybe – that day, you were actually looking where you were going after all.

Sometimes it is the clutter and debris of the storm which makes you see most clearly which direction you are meant to go.

It was possibly the best sunset
I had ever seen.
Spreading out across the white sand.
Red, orange, and yellow.
It took over the horizon,
yet the entire time
I stared only at you.
For you are deeper than
any colour,
shine brighter
than any star,
you are the most
impressive creation
I have ever witnessed.
I no longer need to journey far in
order witness a beautiful view,
because every day
I wake up and simply
look at You.

It was after the first storm of spring – the one that diminishes your hope for warmer days and rips off the brand-new petals that have only just grown. It was the morning after the storm had passed, the winds had died down, and the showers subsided - that moment when you first unlock the back door and step outside. Your feet touch wet wood and dew drops fall on your forehead. Through the fog and empty branches you see it, the first new blossoms on the tree.

Regrown.

That is how it felt when you found me.

Hopeful.

My heart felt like a playground.
Boys had come and gone,
used me for entertainment.
Slid down me,
swung on me,
ran around me.
Then you came and
we sat with me on the seesaw –
you on one end,
me on the other,
bouncing off of each other
requiring the other's body weight to rise and fall.
They played with me.
Then you came,
and you Balanced me.

He asked for a drill,
a hammer,
and nails.
He unbolted,
re-stitched.
Painted over...
re-arranged.
He did not follow the instructions –
didn't simply glue together the broken pieces.
Instead, he designed,
he rebuilt
my broken heart.

Until it was
New.

Until it was
Whole.

Until it was
His.

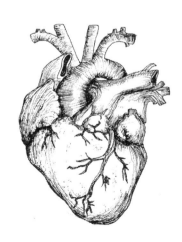

Part Five

THE ADVICE
I NEVER TOOK

Young girls are told never to say "I love you" first. That is supposed to be the boy's job. Perhaps that explains why girls struggle with self-love because we grow up believing that to have love in our lives, someone else has to recognise it first.

A fatal mistake.

Love yourself as much as you love other people.

If you've given it your all and it hasn't worked out, give it time.

If you choose to ignore a lesson, it will come back in a different form … from a different angle … with a different face and a different laugh … again and again until you realise you have something to learn which you've refused to study. And until you do, your lesson will make sure you continue to fail.

Face the consequences.

Don't give your sweet spots to sour people.

You wake the sun up before its alarm ... turn the stars on like a light switch ... your ideas change the clockwork of the tides ... each thought sprinkles mountains with fresh snow ... your energy is as contagious as yawns ... the universe beats for you ... and every part of existence wants you to win despite the fact that you're at a loss right now.

I filled three balloons. One with high standards, the other with expectations, and the last with the pressure I put on myself. But even with three giant balloons, my feet never left the ground. The sun glared in my eyes as I stared up at them. I wished and waited and hoped that they'd hurtle me toward the sky. One day, my fingers grew especially raw. They slowly uncurled from the strings, and I let them go. Clarity began to fall into my lap. Between my fourth finger and thumb, I popped the balloons and felt my lightest yet.

You'll blink your eyes, and your best friend will have a baby. You'll be working at the job you applied for. You'll blink and be shaking the hand of your professor as you graduate with your degree. You'll have a one-way flight out the small town you hate, and your big dreams will become big plans. Blink, and your friendship group will have changed, you'll be more comfortable in your own skin, and your relationship with your parents will be better. It will all get better. You can blink but just don't miss it all happening because it's all going to – it's all going to happen for you.

You are fresh air in a world that's always holding its breath.

Don't underestimate yourself.

Don't worry too much if you failed that paper,
for your most pivotal enrolment is in life.

"People will tell you how to live your life, but they won't give you an instruction manual."

You've got an awful fear of flying for a girl with her head in the clouds.

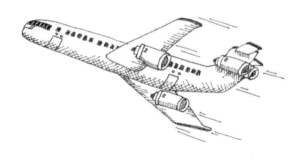

Even if the love in your life is senseless and comes at a cost, see it through. Sneak out of the window that unlocks quietly in the laundry, and drive to his house in your mum's car. Text him first and tell him what you want to do to him. Leave the party and get an Uber to wherever he is. Lose yourself in his smile and never come home. If he breaks your heart, give him a second chance even though it's just going to happen again. Cave in and sleep with your ex because you haven't stopped thinking about him for seven months.

Look here's what I know about you (yes, from my screen in my room as a stranger who has never met you), I know there is someone in this universe who understands you better than anyone else ever has, someone who makes you feel things you've never felt, someone who hears the things you haven't said, and someone who will always be the person you want more than any other human being. That person used to be your partner in crime and now they're not, and that eats you up. Without them you are stumbling in the dark. I know you're scared of the future without them and of the reality that is their absence. The reality of getting rejected when you ask to give it another go. You're scared because this thing you've got going on, well it's an important thing - and for the person you are becoming, it's important that you experience it.

It's important to be terrified in life and terrified in love. Right now, all you want is one person and when there's something you really want with all your heart, peruse it, make it yours, fight for it... and don't give up on it – even if that something or someone has broken you and smashed you to pieces. You still love them, and if it doesn't work out you still want to know that you did everything you could to give it another go.

So ... love them harder, forgive them entirely, and be torn apart again, but even more ruthlessly because the best loves don't come without chaos and they don't happen without bravery.

If there's one thing I know, it's that the most passionate moments in my life have come from taking chances, not from being sensible. They've come from running down the road and jumping into his arms in the pouring rain. They've come from booking the hotel room. They've come from saying yes. They've come from admitting to someone that they have me right where they want me.

The right time is now. Say it. Say the things that you're holding back. Scream it in their face. Tell them you love them more than life itself. Hold your breath and open your heart. Do it. Do it now.

You'll regret it if you don't.

A brief reminder that friendship is not a contract. You do not have to apply for leave. You do not have to give two weeks' notice before resigning. You also do not need a specific event to occur in order to quit. If someone is draining your time, energy, and love, that is reason enough to get out of there. Do not wait to feel a stab in your back when your gut has already told you a certain someone is holding a knife. Trust yourself and what you know will be best for you. I can guarantee you, it is far more beneficial to be alone than it is to be chained to a situation that you feel obliged to be in. Friendship is a choice – every day. It is not a signed form.

You do not owe anyone, anything, ever.
Act accordingly.

You're meant to be friends with the wrong people – the ones who whisper behind your back, drive to school without you, and don't invite you to parties. It's really important that you have a stage of being friends with people who treat you like dirt … who turn their backs to you when they talk and forget the date of your birthday. It's the people like that who make you realise how important empathy is … how important compassion is … how important it is to listen when people speak. It is those friends that make sure you never forget to include anyone and go out of your way to make people feel better about themselves because you know how shitty it is to feel invisible. Without those friends, you wouldn't know what kind of people you like and what you value. It is the friends who may as well be enemies that attract you to the right people. Your right people are out there. Take this time to learn from the wrong ones.

Your facade is fantastic.

Especially the fake focus you pretend to apply to your career; "I'm just doing me right now" and "I'm super goal orientated." The lies flow effortlessly.

Your stomach is empty, and it misses the butterflies. It's been too long. You're good at being alone kid, in fact, you are great, but listen closely, you don't have to be. You don't have to sit at tables, catch buses and walk home in the rain alone. You're allowed to say you want to find someone. It doesn't make you weak. Sure, it makes you vulnerable but vulnerability is the portal to how souls connect. Everyone has gentle spots. They are not something to spend your life ignoring. You do not have to plaster yours in so that you appear to a poster of happy perfection to the outside world.

You are allowed to see a couple resting their heads on each other and say "I miss that." You are allowed to feel that emptiness prick your lonely fingers.

That feeling that is just your heart showing you what you want. Someone.

You want someone who helps you take the sting of life away.

You're allowed to admit that.

It is okay if nothing is going to plan, it is okay if it all feels wrong if you feel hopeless, purposeless, lost and alone. It is okay if you are in tears before you've had your morning coffee. You might be reading this with no idea of what is going to happen or if anything is ever going to get better. You might cry yourself to sleep tonight, or my personal favourite, you might scream at the world for everything it's putting you through.

Trust me when I tell you, it does it get better. Your passion will find you, your people find you, and you will find your place. You will look back on this time of your life as if you are putting on an old dress with its stitching undone and its fit too small. You will have outgrown it – developed into something far better than you can imagine.

You will have taught yourself that through committing to consistency and love, you've made it through. Forget the excuses and stop feeling sorry for yourself. It is time to gather your strength. It is time to fight back. It is time to wake up and go after what you want. You do not need to be saved. You do not need a knight to rescue you.

Look down – it is you who is wearing the shining armour.

The things you should do are the things that never come to you. You have to go to them.

In case you don't know this, you have those eyes – you know, those beautiful big eyes. They shine because there are light bulbs behind them. You've got those good ideas. You can see things. In case no one's told you this, you should trust yourself – trust those ideas.

They are going to take you places.

You are a good person. However, there are bad people out there, and you are giving out forgiveness like cookies.

Be careful. Some people are greedy.

You lock the front door to your house yet let anyone inside your body.

What makes the two any different?

Protect yourself.

Write her a farewell card, sign your name with kisses, lick the envelope closed, and add a stamp. She is memorable and special, but her time is up. She is not the person you're meant to be anymore. You're upgrading – getting faster, sharper, harder, smarter, and with longer hair. For this upgrade, the old model must be retired – say goodbye to her, kiss her on the cheek, thank her, tell her you'll never forget her, and put the envelope in the postage box. Now grow – grow upwards.

When each possible domino that could have fallen fell, a close friend reminded me that life is like a jewellery box. Even when all the necklaces get tangled, it doesn't make them any less beautiful. The diamonds don't shine any less brightly, and it's as simple to fix as the un-doing of a clasp.

Things are still beautiful when they are messed up.

Don't eat all day. Skip meals to hear your stomach grumble to confirm that your body feels as hollow as your heart. Keep trying to be something you're not – dye your hair then cut it short … add accessories to what you've naturally got, like acrylic nails or eyelash extensions. Cover up your natural style with clothes that are in fashion right now. Test out the quick fix – what diet can you go on to drop five pounds in five seconds? Compliment your empty stomach with dark eyeshadow and buy a large bottle of vodka. Drink it too fast … drink too much … don't think about the repercussions of your behaviour. Swing it back until you're face-first down a toilet, holding onto the sides of the bowl with every bit of sanity you have left. Stare down the barrel and confess to yourself how alone you honestly feel. Let your world spin until you can't remember which way is up. Try and vomit out every bit of dissatisfaction you have. Do whatever you can to eradicate who you are from existence. Harm yourself and lose control just so that at the end of the night when you can't hold your body weight up, your arms are shaking and your stomach is heaving. You will clutch onto the side of the bed, praying for nothing but to feel yourself again … to open your eyes to feel the harmony of your heart, blood, and skin … to be you. Find something that makes you feel helpless, and then you will realise how strong you indeed are – you will realise what you can handle. Get it all wrong just so that you can figure it all out.

You'll figure out that you're perfect – just as you are.

Life is not about getting your permission slip signed by your dad to attend the school field trip. It's about organizing your own adventure, not being impacted by opinions, and not relying on anyone to tell you whether or not you can go.

Life is being your own approval.

The Plum Tree

In the back of my garden is a Plum Tree. It holds the rope from my favourite swing when I was three. Across from that is the biggest branch (which was the only one strong enough to hold me and all my cousins). Every morning, my parents have breakfast together. I asked my mum why she always sits in the same seat, and she answered,

"So I can see the Plum Tree!"

But I always forget about the Plum Tree.In winter, the Plum Tree gets especially hidden. It morphs into the grey clouds and gets shaken in sub-zero storms. But after the weather has passed, something incredible happens. Come spring, the Plum Tree teaches me (and anyone else watching) to believe in magic. And just like everything good happens, I swear it changes overnight. I walk out one morning, and it is covered from head to toe in pink and white baby blossoms!

On a rainy spring day this year, my grandma and I sat and looked at the tree. We watched the blossoms twist and plummet to the ground in the wind and rain. I said how awful it was that they were falling off the tree.

Nana smiled, *"No, it's wonderful. They look like confetti!"*

I looked out at the garden again, and I realised she was right! It was beautiful! It was like our whole little garden and the fences and bushes were covered in a thick layer of pink and white confetti! To make it even better, I looked outside again the next morning, and the Plum Tree had grown brand-new baby blossoms overnight.

I realised that the Plum Tree hadn't just taught me to believe in the magic of growth. It had taught me something else as well.

There is always good to come out of bad situations. A simple change of perspective means you can go from seeing awful things to seeing amazing things. It simply depends on how you are looking at something. I now know that it is natural for things to get shaken, broken, fall apart, fall off, crunch, crack, and *explode*.

Of course, things need to explode

– how else would confetti be released?

You've got to stop making excuses.
You've got to focus on the right things.
You've got to change your energy.
No one's going to do it for you.
You've got to push yourself,
push yourself over the edge.

And then you've got to open your own parachute.

Criticism isn't personal. Your mother telling you not to eat that biscuit isn't because she thinks you're fat. It's because she's been self-conscious of her weight for years. When your boss says you could have done that differently, it is only because she's seen it work well that way in the past. That stranger's back-handed compliment which left a sting came after three glasses of red wine. Your friend is happy that you went on a hot date – but she isn't reflecting that overly well because she broke up with her boyfriend last night. He does like your hair shorter – he's just used to it long.

A person's opinion is formed from their thought processes, which are formed from their history, their life experiences, and their pains, strains, broken bones, and dreams – none of which have anything to do with you. You don't order steak just because your friend does – maybe you get pizza or pasta or chicken. Why? Because you order what you want, not what someone else wants you to have. Words are mere reflections of someone's past and present. They are not reflections of you.

Put your shield up – deflect them. Opinions can be blocked.

They don't have to be arrows to your soul.

Don't be impressionable. Don't change to fit in.
Don't do something because someone else is.
Don't like something because everyone else does.
Sheep follow each other onto the butcher's truck.

Being different is cool, being passionate is cool,
being odd is coo, having no friends is cool,
struggling with self-love is cool, good grades is
cool, dropping out is cool, reading books is cool,
fitting in is cool, standing out is cool, being self-
conscious is cool, having sex is cool, and being a
virgin is cool.

Everyone's a cool kid.

No one is better than anyone else, okay?

Everybody has a treasure chest in them – they just have to have the confidence to unlock it.

Why do you think you are not creative when you've created yourself this entire time?

At the end of the day, you will lie down in bed alone, regardless of how many friends you have, if your parents are together, what job have, if you achieved your goals, if you're in your hometown, or if you've moved countries. No matter what, you will still go home to an empty house, and you must face the fact that no one gave enough of a shit to stick around to be there. No one loved you as much as you loved them.

You have a bucket inside you … a bucket you long to be filled, and people can fill it up just as quickly as they can pour it out. Don't expect situations or people to give you fulfilment. They don't owe it to you, and they won't give it to you. They'll play with you, they'll make splashes or tidal waves in your bucket, and then they will leave you incomplete and unfulfilled. They'll take it away just as fast as they give it.

But that's okay – it's your bucket, and you choose how deep it goes.

Circus

I tightened the Velcro on my gloves. It was incredibly important to have a tight grip around my wrists for the trapeze act. Genetically, I had small hands which made it tough to grab the bars without support. Luckily, I wasn't on my own in this. I had him, and he had my back. He was an incredible circus performer – truly talented. He could spin and drive and fly and twirl like you've never seen before. Sometimes when he breathed fire and his teeth glistened under the disco ball, I didn't even believe he was human.

"You're on in five."

I was sixteen when I ran away from home to be with the circus. There was not a day that went by that I didn't miss my family, but I knew I'd taken the skills they taught me and applied them to the real world. I could hear the crowd getting louder and louder as I walked out from backstage. The flashes from people's cameras looked like strobe lights. The lion's roar from the previous act shook the tent. My cheeks got hotter, my hands got sweatier, and my leotard got tighter. The velvet curtain sprang open. Ahead of me was the podium I dove from. It was simple metal, and from it lay a plain wooden bar – nothing fancy, a smooth wooden bar connected to two incredibly long wires. The music started, and to perfect timing, I hurtled myself gracefully off the podium. Just like I'd always done, I flew through the air to the timing of everyone's applause. I made sure not to get lost in the moment, and I kept my eyes opened to catch his gaze. He would grab my feet and swing me to the other platform, dropping me off and completing a somersault on the way back. I couldn't see him. Where was he? Had he realised we were meeting at this time? Had he not seen on the roster that he was performing? Did he not want to catch me? Had he forgotten about me?

Those long wires started swinging faster. I picked up pace. That wooden bar got slippery and even more slippery. With one heart-wrenching rip, the Velcro I'd been so careful to do up earlier just couldn't hold on any longer. I couldn't hold on any longer. I needed him to let go. And with that I fell.

A silent fall.

Slow yet fast, long yet short. I fell 45 feet down in the air. The impact of my fall was winding – like someone had knocked every bit of air out of my lungs, sense from my brains, and love from my heart. I lay motionless and paralysed, and as I came to my senses, all I could notice was a deafening sound. But instead of the gasps and cries that I was expecting, I only heard cheers, hoorays, screaming, clapping, banging, and fireworks going off. I looked up through the dust, dirt, and blood dripping into my eyes. It was through the glaze and haze that I saw it.

I saw him.

Hurtling through the air, launching off his platform – twisting and turning and somersaulting, just like I told you he could. He had timed the performance so everyone would watch his spectacular show whilst I fell into darkness. He had timed it so he was in the spotlight. The hero. The superstar. All the attention on him. The compliments and praise given to the guy who was only able to do that trick because I had set it up. He had used me, abused me, hurt me, and left me anxious and unable to trust again – scared and injured. He had taken what I held close to me – what I loved – and used it against me for his own pleasure. He had used my talent, my body, and my assets to help him with what he needed. How dull to have to abuse someone else in order to shine. I wonder if he felt guilty for using me? I wonder if he ever told anyone what he'd done? I wonder if he ever thought about it and regretted it? I wonder if he ever knew how much confidence he'd knocked out of me that night?

It was from the dust, dirt, and blood that I dragged myself away, cleaned my own cuts, and covered my own scars. It was from this pain that he had caused me that I found the pleasure I could form within myself. After that, I left that circus and started a new one – my own circus where the performances were on my terms along with the animals and the staging. I wonder if perhaps one day he'll find himself as an audience member at my sold-out show and see me perform that jump. But this time, I would do it without him. After that incident, I learned the only person I can rely on and trust is myself. So, I learned to do it alone. I didn't need anyone else to hold on to. I could let go by myself.

BULLY

I was sixteen when I ran away to the circus.

And I was sixteen when a man first touched me against my will.

Down that road three years ago and pressed
against the side of the building, my voice was not
as loud as my mind.

You see, even bricks melt down to concrete, and
you melted me down until I was small enough
for you to fulfil your needs ... to fit in the back
pocket of your unzipped jeans. I did not consent
to your body on top of mine nor to your fingers
inside me, but I must not let that put me off
being underneath another man now.

It is not his fault that my organs are locked up in
chains and coated with doubt – it is yours.

I have always loved fairy tales. I always thought they taught me lessons of hope, love, and happy endings. I remember a nightlight I had when I was younger. It was a globe nightlight that revolved constantly. On it was a story of a fire-breathing dragon, a princess that was captured and held in a cave, and a prince trying to slay the dragon. At different times in my life, I have been all three of these characters that circled my nightlight as a child. However, they did not just teach me lessons of love. I now realise they taught me about life. All good things require work, and good things challenge you. Sometimes, to get to what you most want, you have to slay the evil dragon in front of it. Sometimes, when you find something that fills you with light, you have to breathe fire on the intruders and the thieves in order to protect it. Sometimes as a girl, men want to take you. Grab you. Change you. Contain you. Manipulate you. You need to create your own strategy. You need to stand up for yourself. My prayer for you, princess, is that you are the dragon. I pray when you walk the ground shakes. I pray you have the power to stand up against any man or ideal of what he thinks you should be. I hope you terrify the soul of every doubter. I pray you fight for what you love, and I pray, my princess, that your fire never goes out.

Don't believe everything you hear, especially when it's you who's saying it.

Show off – it's okay. Talk about your achievements with pride. Say, "I worked hard for this." Say, "I earned this." Say, "I deserve this." You value yourself. Don't make your wins look like losses because other people are just sore losers.

You can do everything a man can – always. You can be feminine and masculine. You can be a boss ... wear the pants ... call the shots ... get to the top ... get *on* top. Never let anyone prioritise someone else just because of their gender. Speak up.

Our generation is scrolling instead of looking. We are trapped in apps and bright whites. Our view on relationships is saturated by VSCO Cam filters. We are idolising strangers' relationships from afar without knowing what is truly happening in their lives. You can see two people smiling online, but that doesn't mean they are happy together. We've got a generation that confuses likes for love, and we need to do something about it. Liking your photo, replying to your story, following you back, adding you on Facebook, or forming a snapchat streak does not indicate someone's affection for you. Actions speak louder than online attention. Pay attention to how someone else treats you in reality – not virtually. Do they hold your hand when you're walking down the street? Remember your favourite café for breakfast? Wake you up with kisses? Call to see if you got home safe? We are mistaking feelings for iPhone notifications.

To a generation that's scrolling – look up.

You recognize vodka because you've tasted water. The strong stuff makes you appreciate the gentle stuff – you appreciate happiness because you have tasted despair.

You have to think it into existence.

Happiness.

Don't compare your productivity, job, car, education, qualifications, experience, CV, or bank account to anyone else's. I'll tell you a secret ... no one's as successful, happy, or rich as they pretend to be.

The people who act like they have it all tend to be the people who have nothing.

Nothing matters as much as you think it does. It doesn't matter if you wear a skirt or if you wear pants. It doesn't matter if you drink or sober drive. It doesn't matter if you had an extra coffee today. It doesn't matter if you spent your pay check on an outfit you'll only wear once. It doesn't matter if you're complaining too much. It doesn't matter if you go to the party alone. We worry over what went wrong and what we should have done. What matters is whether or not you jumped into the pool or stayed on the edge … if you were curious. What matters is what you did for others … what you did to give back. What matters is how much you loved. What matters is if you found your freedom. What matters is what you learnt and how you changed.

In the end, what matters is how imperfectly perfect your life was.

She might have a smaller frame ... you might be curvier. She might have acne ... you might have clearer skin. She might have brown hair, and you're blonde. She might have a straighter nose, and you might have a big forehead. She might have a job, but you might have a degree. But none of this matters because she is drop-dead gorgeous, and you are so breathtakingly beautiful that flowers bloom when your eyes open. To spend your time focusing on what you don't have is wasting time that should be spent being grateful for what you do have. There is no better and no greater than right now. Turn your attention inward instead of outward and see what you find – it might just be everything you've been looking for.

Even when you are deflated, inflate others.

Nothing is out of your league. Give the cute guy your number. Apply for the job. Ask for a promotion or a raise. Introduce yourself to your boss's boss. Invite the new girl out for lunch. Take the dance class. Enrol in those night classes. Stand up for the quiet kid. Complain when your order is wrong. Don't settle for that haircut. Get the right change. Be good to people. Ask for favours when you need them. Ask questions. Don't hold yourself back.

Be careful what you say to yourself – the universe is eavesdropping.

Respect your elders.

They told me they know best. They ran their hands over my ideas and gasped as my razor blades cut them. They were not wearing their glasses. They couldn't see my vision or understand my future. They told me to delete the curse words and take out anything that mentioned sex. I never understood why they always told me that sexuality, sexual assault, and sex should be whispered about. I think it should be screamed about. I respected the integrity of their history, but I also respect myself. I will not bow down to what they claim to be correct because they cannot see what I can. I can see a generation starving to feel accepted. I was right to do this on my own, to make it without them. I do not need the hand of experience to be successful. To me, success is holding the hand of my youngest reader through my own words. I will swear if I want to. I will talk about sex when I need to.

I will make sure every ethnicity, religion, gender, sexuality, and identity that comprises the souls which read my writing feel passionately accepted here. Because they are.

I will respect my elders, but I will not respect the people who tried to change my words, cut my words, harness my words, put padlocks on them, dehydrate them, and lock them up. They are not yours to keep. They are mine, and they are not for you. They are for the one reading this.

Hey angel, you should test out those wings on your back.

Dear Future Self,

You are writing this at your kitchen table at the end of one of the most eye-opening years of your life. I don't know where you will be when you open this. I don't know if you'll be 21 or 31, but if you've opened this, I assume something has gone right. I don't know if you're in New Zealand or not, but I really hope that by the time you read this, you feel how I feel right now — proud. I hope you have jumped into life with both feet first. I hope you're still writing. I hope people are reading your writing. I hope you've found a way to heal people. I hope you're looking after yourself and proving everyone wrong. I hope you've found someone who loves you as much as you love them. I hope when you see "his" name, all you will think about is a girl who learnt an incredible lesson. You are so courageous, but you're equally as scared. You'll always be that girl, and that's okay. I hope you've stayed strong. I hope you've had the balls to apply for any job you want, and I hope you smashed it out of the park. I hope you applied for that VISA, made that change, and moved countries. I hope it changed your life. I hope you have left toxic people in your dust. I hope your relationship with yourself has healed. I hope your relationship with food is better. I hope your anxiety is quiet. You are so unique and have so much to offer. I pray that you have given people the opportunity to learn from you. I hope you've spent your time writing, reading, and doing things you love. I hope you're settled and happy. I hope you feel yourself. I hope you took every risk, jumped every fence, kissed every boy, fell in love, saw some shit, laughed till you cried, found your feet, and found your tribe of people. I love you so much – I always have, and I always will. I'm sorry for what I put you through growing up. I hope you made up for it. Actually, I'll re-word that. I *know* we have made up for it.

Love,

Cass xx

written October 14th 2016,
opened October 14th 2018.

Opened when everything I
had wished for, came true.

Stop beating yourself up.

Bully

Perhaps these pages have shown you that your demon is not such a bad thing after all. She knows everything about you, and believe it or not, with her ability to pick out your greatest vulnerabilities, she is actually highlighting your greatest strengths. The stories you have just read have been written since I was 14. I tried to write anxiety, bulimia, and heartbreak away, but I did not know I was writing the greatest masterpiece of my life. It is because of them that you have read this book. Do not forget – a boat ride without waves, a rollercoaster without twists, a flower without falling petals, and a car without speed would be boring. It is tricky chapters that make you interesting.

So, what are you meant to do if the bully is in your head?

Didn't they ever tell you to keep your friends close and your enemies closer?

To everyone who has ever broken my heart - including myself. Thank you for being my teacher, for without your lessons my words would still be lost.

And to everyone who helped me put the pieces back together - my family and friends, thank you for inspiring me to keep going even when it felt like the only option was to give up.

I would tell you about the author but there is nothing left to say. You have opened her ligaments, torn her skin and read her heart…page by page, cover to cover. And now you know her better than I do, but in all honesty I don't think anybody really knows her at all. She's a lone wolf, she's a conspiracy, a wanderer, a day dream, an unsolved case and she's never in one place for long. You've probably seen her in a dusty bookstore flicking through poetry, at a café eating breakfast alone, sitting at the front of the bus or on someone's shoulders at a festival high on life. She's twenty people in one. She's always thinking. She's always moving. If you squint carefully you might see her wings, they used to be tight and tender, but now she flexes them proudly. I haven't spoken to her recently, but she's very grateful for you. She wants you to know she loves you - all the way from the other side of the world, from a New York sky scrapper, from the rolling hills of Italy, from the shores of New Zealand, from the stacks of stars above us – she loves you… to the moon and back. She always will.

For more from Cassandra...

@cassgrodd

@quoteswithcass

A special thank you to my dear friend Raaya for her illustrations. Raaya, you truly brought my words to life.

For more of her work:

@by.raaya.

95425956R00160

Made in the USA
San Bernardino, CA
16 November 2018